Flight of the Wild Geese

Flight of the
Wild Geese

Graham Uney

Whittles Publishing

Published by
Whittles Publishing,
Dunbeath,
Caithness KW6 6EY,
Scotland, UK
www.whittlespublishing.com

© 2008 Graham Uney

ISBN 978-1904445-54-8

Typeset by Ellipsis Books Limited, Glasgow

Printed by Dardedze Holography, Riga, Latvia

Contents

Acknowledgements

To my Livi, for making it all possible, and lots of fun, and also to my brother Dave, for always managing to fall into bogs or ponds whenever we go out, and so making the most dreich of days worth getting out of bed for.

There are other people I should like to thank, starting with the rest of my family for at least trying to understand my obsession with wildlife and the 'cold north'. Also Beryl and Dick Tudhope for sharing walks, wine and single malt whisky, and much more besides. Thanks also to Janet Fisher for her inspiration, and for not looking too bored when I waffle on about our wildlife.

On a more technical note, I would like to express my gratitude to Gabrielle Dean of World Expeditions for arranging my trip to Spitsbergen with Oceanwide Expeditions. Also, to Paramo for providing suitable clothing for me to wear in the Arctic and on the Solway. I wouldn't be without it now! I would also like to say thanks to Dr Larry Griffin of the Wildfowl and Wetlands Trust, and to the RSPB for their support and technical advice regarding barnacle geese and the wildlife of the Solway.

Thanks also to all at Whittles Publishing for seeing this project through to the end. You've all done a great job!

Foreword

All books strive to compress space and time between their covers and this book does it admirably well whether scaling from a trip to the local patch to see familiar birds in familiar settings or when sailing on a trip of a lifetime to see cherished birds in more exotic settings. When I opened this book, the stories and descriptions expanded to link in with my own remembrances of wildlife watching, the desire to go north (from London to Scotland) and what it is like to live and work on the Solway and in the Arctic, especially with iconic species such as the barnacle goose.

I suspect that most people reading this book will recognise at least some elements of their own experiences and as such it is a useful aide-memoire as to why we are doing what we are doing and why we are where we are. Like an impressionist, the author daubs colour and sound here and there to evoke the landscapes of the Solway and the Arctic, among others, and images of the birds that many will admire or will now wish to know.

Dr Larry Griffin
Senior Research Officer, WWT Caerlaverock Wetland Centre
Dumfriesshire, Scotland DG1 4RS.

Preface

This is much more than a book about barnacle geese. This book is about the winter wildlife of the Solway Firth, that glorious estuary set between the hills of Cumbria and Dumfries and Galloway, and the links they share with the islands of the North Atlantic and the High Arctic.

It is also about a journey through life, from humble beginnings in East Yorkshire, growing to appreciate the wildlife of our wild places, and a yearning to know more about where our winter birds go during the summer.

I hope you enjoy reading about the wonderful, wild landscapes of the Solway, the isolated islands of Scotland, the North Atlantic and the Arctic, and the wildlife that connects these places, as much as I have enjoyed following my passion for nature and life in the north.

Graham Uney
Hertfordshire

1

Arriving from the Arctic

A quiet rustle of wind moved through the reeds, easily parting them with its cold breath and finding the goose-pimpled skin on my exposed face and arms. Little other movement stirred through the expanse of marsh, other than faint dimples in the inky flats as a few late, lingering insects of summer dipped into the dark waters.

Movement may have been hardly discernible in the still autumn evening, but sounds there were aplenty. Far out across the huge expansive flatness of gently swaying brown reeds, an occasional, slightly comic whistle carried on the still air to where I stood. I'd not heard this surprised-sounding bird call for a long time, and although I knew it well enough, the long days of summer had dulled my awareness and familiarity of the bird that uttered it. It took me a few seconds to recognise the once-familiar high-pitched call. The wild wigeon had begun to return to the shores of the Solway for the winter.

I edged carefully along the grassy verge which fringes the marsh here, following it beneath a canopy of low hawthorns and elders. The trees and gorse bushes alongside the little road provided a screen, and led towards the western end of the marsh. Here an open stretch of water can be viewed from the grassy bank. I sat on the dewy ground and scanned through the fading light with my binoculars. Dark shapes moved on the flats, but it was more of an audio experience than a visual one, and I could hear an occasional 'wheeeeeee', dropping in tone as it rushed out from the bill of a freshly arrived wigeon.

Looking out across the shimmering expanse of water, I could just make out the silhouetted outline of the birds in the gathering blackness, but it was by now far too dark to gather any impression of their bright colours. They bow-waved serenely through the darkly glistening levels, and I could pick out the sharp-edged shape of 20 or more ducks.

The autumn brings many birds to the Solway Firth. As the cold creeps down from the north, poking icy fingers into the thin, gritty soil of the Arctic tundra, the vegetation becomes covered with a fresh layer of snow. This sparse vegetation is naturally close-cropped by the biting harshness of the frost and ice, and also by the hundreds of thousands of grazing birds that feed here during the summer. The birds that feed, mate and nest here – waders, ducks, geese, and swans – find that, come the autumn, their herbaceous food supply is getting a bit thin on the ground, so to speak. At first, they dig through the soft powder snow to reach the dying shoots. This tactic works for a few days, but then the snow consolidates into hard névé, snow too tough for the birds to dig or probe into, so they move south, the advancing winter to their backs.

They come in their thousands, skeins of 'V's cutting across the autumn sky. Some move down the North Sea coast of Scandinavia and filter out into the flatlands of Denmark and Holland, or cross the sea itself to find warmer, greener pastures in Britain.

These wigeon at Campfield Marsh, a little-visited RSPB reserve on the southern, Cumbrian shores of the Solway, were among the very first of these new arrivals. Certainly, they were the first I'd seen that autumn. The 20 or so individuals whistling into the cold night before me had just made a phenomenal journey. A journey in search of food. A journey of survival. But that's only part of the miracle of migration. Hundreds of thousands of birds were following in their wing-beats, or at least were busily feeding up, preparing for the adventure.

I walked back along the road to where I'd parked the car on the outskirts of the little village of Bowness-on-Solway, and then drove the short distance home to Brampton, the small market town tucked into the northern flanks of the most northerly reaches of the Pennine chain.

It was not all wigeon out there on the Solway. Over the next few days other species would arrive too. The small numbers of teal – diminutive little dabbling ducks sporting bright green swirls across the sides of their ruddy-coloured heads – that breed on the Solway during the summer are joined by their northern kin in their thousands. Pintail ducks, heads all chocolatey and dapper, fly in alongside pochards, mallards, gadwall and shovelers. Bigger and more impressive still, whooper and Bewick's swans angle in over the open water, delicate and almost balletic, then crash clumsily onto the surface, throwing spumes of water before their black, outstretched webbed feet.

These birds can be seen at lots of stretches of open water around the northern part of Britain (although far fewer than previously in the case of the Bewick's swans), but there is one particular bird that likes the wide expanses of the Solway Firth to such an extent that it pretty much refuses to spend the cold months anywhere else. The barnacle goose is a bit of a stickler for tradition. There are three very distinct and very separate populations of barnacle geese in the world. They breed in three different regions and hardly ever mix with birds from the other groups.

Greenland has one large breeding population, and during the winter, when these birds are in Britain, they spread out along the west coast. Huge numbers descend on the lovely Scottish island of Islay, just off the coast of Argyll, while other members of the Greenland flock fly to the wild islands of Orkney, the Outer Hebrides or the west coast of Ireland. The odd thing here is that the entire Greenland population of barnacle geese chooses to spend the winter in Britain. They choose Britain exclusively.

This strange liking for British soil is not confined to the Greenland population though. Another of the three groups of barnacle geese find their summer homes on the Arctic tundra of Svalbard, the tight archipelago way up north of Norway, and these spend the winter pretty much entirely on the Solway Firth, between Dumfries and Galloway in Scotland and Cumbria in England.

So, as I drove home that night, with the memory of the cool darkness creeping along the shores of the Solway and of the sound of a wind orchestra of ducks, geese and swans honking and brattling into the night, I knew that part of that orchestra had been made up of a few thousand sprucely tuxedoed barnacle geese. I also knew where these geese had come from: the cold, barren regions of Svalbard.

A few days later I returned to the Solway with my older brother, Dave. He'd travelled up from East Yorkshire for a few days, and while we'd planned to spend part of the time tracking down black grouse in the North Pennines, red kites in Galloway and mountain hares in the Moorfoot Hills of Scotland, we also had a day out on the Scottish side of the Solway in our sights. Dave runs his own business as an auto-electrician, but would dearly love to pursue a new career as a wildlife photographer. We often get together to go out stalking unsuspecting birds, mammals and insects with our cameras, to varying degrees of success, it has to be said.

Wind howled across the brown, fast-flowing waters of the Esk as we crossed the bridge at Longtown, just south of the Scottish border. As you cross this great red, fell-sandstone structure over the river, you get a good look along its course to the east to where it emerges from around a big bend. Shingle banks hold pairs of oystercatchers here, and in the summer common sandpipers nest down among the rocks, while herons fish the shallows and sand martins pluck flies from the gentle summer breezes. It couldn't have been more different on that autumn day though. The banks on either side were brimming with brown water, each surge topped with a dirty, peat-stained crest. Willow trees – usually growing along the banks, but now well and truly in midstream – bent almost to the point of cracking, while way out to the west, in the direction of the Solway, a ragged skein of geese were being thrown around the skies as they desperately dropped wings in an effort to lose height. We lost sight of the geese as they descended, but knew that they'd probably come to land on the vast expanses of Rockcliffe Marsh.

Rockcliffe Marsh is a huge area of saltflats, not far from where I lived. A peninsula jutting out into the head of the Solway, Rockcliffe acts as a vast feeding ground for lots of birds in the winter, as a gathering ground for barnacle geese prior to their departure for the Arctic at the start of summer, and as a breeding ground for thousands of gulls in the summer. With the great waters of the River Esk on its north side and the equally copious waters of the River Eden on its south, it's an important natural landmark on the estuary.

The Esk brings waters down from the Southern Uplands of the Scottish Borders, and this impressive river drains a very large area of this hill region. The Eden is very similar in character, rising high on Mallerstang Common way up on the northern edge of the Yorkshire Dales National Park and flowing through the western fringes of the Pennines, lapping the buildings of the city of Carlisle, sometimes a little too closely for comfort, before emptying into the Solway basin.

As Dave and I drove northwards into Scotland, we passed the large gravel pits that lie close to the north-western fringes of Longtown. These scrapes are now disused and flooded and provide a great little wildlife habitat for mute swans, geese, ducks and gulls that use the area to feed during the winter. Black-headed gulls rose on the wind and were carried 20 or 30 feet in the air before managing to drop back onto the choppy surface below.

Heading west along the road, we crossed the motorway via the flyover, and the extra height gained gave us a brief opportunity to survey the openness of the flood plains that lie all around. We stopped briefly and had a scan with the binoculars, first picking out a small wintering flock of redwings and fieldfares in nearby hawthorn hedges. Beyond these, though, out in the distance, we could now see the growing gaggle of barnacle geese, busily grazing on Rockcliffe Marsh. There were perhaps a hundred in total, and others came by in their twos and threes, ducking violently between gusts, and all but crash-landing among the flustered looking flock.

A few whooper swans were also feeding there, and we wondered if there was any point in driving onwards to Caerlaverock on such a wild day, when we could easily amuse ourselves nearer at hand on the marsh. However, there's usually a good selection of other wildlife over on this northern flank of the Solway, so we continued westwards.

Caerlaverock Wildfowl and Wetlands Trust reserve was, not surprisingly, very quiet, at least from a visitor point of view, both human and avian. Howling gales battered the old farm buildings that today house the visitor centre, a small café and the various staff offices. Leaves, now brown and dry, rushed hither and thither on the pelting wind, and few visitors had bothered to turn out on such a wicked and obnoxious day.

We started by climbing to the top of the Tower Hide, a tall structure rising abruptly from the old farmhouse building. A series of stone stairs leads up to the top floor, where a cold and draughty observation room gives fine views across most of the reserve. We shivered in the hide, while below us white wave crests chased across the waters. Every sheltered bay seemed to be packed with ducks, geese and swans.

Mallards were everywhere, but then they often are, being by far the most numerous duck species in the country. Scattered among the wildly bobbing rafts of these commoners were other, more exotic-looking species, most of which were at Caerlaverock for the relatively warmer winter climate that can be found here, as opposed to that way up in the Arctic.

Tufted ducks were diving in the deeper water, searching out food from the bottoms of the various lakes and scrapes. A few pochards were mixed in with these, adding a bit of colour to the large flocks. These round-looking birds appear to be mid-grey on their backs, sides and wings, but have a closer look in good light and you suddenly realise that they have a wonderful dark russet head. Like tufted ducks, pochards are also members of the group known as diving ducks. They plunge below the surface and usually stay under for a good half-minute or so, searching out plant material for food, and also the occasional aquatic beastie that they may come across if they are lucky.

Whooper swans at Caerlaverock

5

There are two main groups of ducks, with one or two individual species that refuse to fall into either group. Tufties and pochards are diving ducks, along with ruddy ducks and goldeneyes. The other group, made up of species we are all more used to seeing on shallow village ponds and the like, are known as dabbling ducks. These feed by sieving water through their bills, sifting out crustaceans, plankton and plant deposits. They often do this right on the surface of the water, but they also frequently up-end with their bottoms in the air while they sift mucky water through their bills extended at a slight depth. Mallards are the classic and most familiar of the dabbling ducks, but you can also find teal, gadwall, shovelers and pintails all doing exactly the same thing.

Dave and I watched from the tower hide as a crazy mix of species fed in the sheltered waters, while on land 400–500 wigeon went about their own feeding frenzy. Whereas all geese are adapted to feeding on land, eating mainly grasses, but also digging for roots and tubers, wigeon are the only duck species that do this regularly. Here at Caerlaverock they were really going for it, grazing a large area of pasture and letting out melodious whistling 'wheeoh's as they did so.

There's a long avenue of trees heading eastwards from the farm at Caerlaverock, and I was keen to head out along this to the viewing hides that have been strategically placed at points along its length. To the north of this avenue, discreetly screened from view, there are a number of shallow pools or scrapes. These are often full of waders, such as redshank, curlew and snipe, but I knew that if I wanted to track down the barnacle geese, I'd have to try the hides either on the south side, or right at the far end of the avenue. These all overlook grazing pastures that are ideal for the geese to feed on.

I started at the first hide, leaving Dave to photograph the vivid yellowhammers that swarmed along a hedgerow back near the visitor centre. I ducked low through the gap in the hide side, nothing more than an opening that served as an entrance in the fibreglass wall, and sat quietly down on a rickety wooden bench, then reaching up, turned a clasp that locks the shutter window in place and gingerly dropped it down. A blackbird in a nearby hawthorn tree turned and fled with a loud squawk, dropping the bright red haw on which it had been about to feed, but apart from that, I couldn't see any other birds at all out on the grassy flats.

The next hide revealed the same, except for the lack of a blackbird, and I was beginning to wonder if all the barnacle geese on the Solway were over on the Cumbrian side. So, as I continued eastwards down the wind tunnel formed by the avenue of sycamore trees, I decided to battle on right to the end of the passageway where there is another large tower hide. This would give me an open view of this part of the reserve, right up to the merse lands beside the channel of Lochar Water, the river that cuts in long meanders across the farmland of Dumfries and into the Solway at the eastern fringes of the reserve.

Once at the hide I climbed right up to the top floor, and then positioned myself so that I could scan the surrounding fields with my binoculars. The first thing I picked out, way over to the north was a roe deer, feeding on stubbles by a drainage channel. Drab in his muddy-brown winter coat, he blended in with the surrounding starkness of the fields and seemed almost to cower beneath the graphite skies.

Moving round to the east, my field of view was suddenly filled with a great blur cast against these dark skies. Almost a mist at first, then each individual particle getting larger and more defined, and eventually becoming a bird. A huge flock of geese were heading down the Solway from the direction of Rockcliffe Marsh. They grew more and more distinct as they flew, changing course slightly to aim directly at the hide from which I watched. They dropped inelegantly, each bird frantically wing-dipping, first one side, then the other, to lose height in a battle against the wild wind that seemed to threaten to carry them all the way back to Svalbard.

There could be little doubt about it. Autumn had arrived, and so had the birds of winter.

This is one of the greatest, perhaps *the* greatest, and most exciting times of year for me. There's a rush of excitement at the anticipation of a long, harsh winter. I know it's not for everyone, but winter is by far my favourite season. I love the cold days, when the sky is bright and the foliage of the fields, moors and mountains is coated with a thick layer of hoar frost. I even love those dank days when the clouds sit so low over everything that you begin to wonder if you'll ever actually get to see the sky again. When the winter ends, it seems to merge into spring in a series of dull, often wet, and usually windy days, and although spring is a time of great excitement in the countryside, too, it's just not the same as a good, hard winter. Then the flowers of spring push through the leaf-litter of our woods, emerging from their recently dormant bulbs, rhizomes and corms, and rush us headlong towards summer. The heat and, more and more frequently in recent years, the wetness of summer bring an abundance of flowers and fruits, which herald a time of renewal. Then as we fall towards summer's end, the sun and wind dry everything out, slowly turning leaves and grasses brown as we enter autumn, and I'm about ready for the first snowfall to arrive.

I suppose this is one of the things I really love about Britain. You will probably laugh at this, but I do love the British weather. Olivia and I recently holidayed in Extremadura in central Spain, and while it was a fascinating place to visit, full of improbable castles and great wildlife, the weather was just too much for me. We had a wonderful holiday, but the stifling heat and endless sunshine was all a bit too predictable. I longed for days when you never really know what the weather will bring when you get out of bed to draw the curtains each morning. Or indeed if that weather outside your window will last more than an hour or so. How many times have you got out of bed, peeked out the window and declared that it's raining and horrible, then by the time you've finished breakfast, have been pulling on walking boots to stride out into the sunshine? I adore this uncertainty of our weather, and the fact that it's not the same every single day for weeks on end.

Mountain folk in Britain have a couple of sayings about the weather. One of them goes, 'If you don't like what the weather's doing, just wait five minutes and you'll get something else.' On some days that can certainly be true. Another says that, 'If you can see the mountains, it's going to rain. And if you can't see the mountains, it's raining already.' At times, that can be true too. But at others, when the clouds suddenly peel apart, unwrapping the sun from behind a thick bank of cumulus, you really feel like the great earth-building process has just finished, all the world is cooling before your eyes and new life is about to be revealed for the first time.

However, it is the vivid autumnal splash of colour, when trees are adorned with mad dashes of vermilion, russet, burgundy, scarlet, ochre and yellow, that brings great excitement, to me at least. I just love the feeling that the whole of our world is about to be stripped down to its bare bones, given a thorough wash and blow dry, and hopefully a deep freeze too. Then, a few months down the line, it's all ready to go again, to start afresh the following spring. I always see the autumn as the start of something exhilarating and immense, rather than the sad end to the summer past.

The air is often dry and cold as we enter autumn, and wild crescendos of wind, often straight off the North Sea, sweep down from the Arctic and over our lands, tearing the leaves from the trees and bundling our bodies as we go about our daily business. We always know when autumn's arrived. It's this change, this suddenness, that's so in your face.

Having said that, it's a surprise every year, round about October time, when suddenly I realise that the birds of summer have long gone. When I have to stop and think, 'When did I last see a swallow?' And yes, I suppose there is a little sadness in that too. But suddenly again, there's just no time to mourn the passing south of these swallows, because the air is full of crazy honking geese from the far north, and besides, the swallows will be back when the time is right for them. So for now, let's enjoy these wonderful, slightly bizarre, wild visitors from the north.

2

Natural beginnings

It had rained for most of the week. We'd had a couple of short drives, the whole family crammed into dad's Marina, out across the high roads that cut from dale to dale across the fells, but the cloud had been so low that we'd not even had a glimpse of them from the fug of the car. We knew these fells were there, though, the great, lumbering beds of limestone and gritstone, piled one stratum atop the other, and topped with peat. Over millennia, these beds had been smoothed off, flanks and crown, by the glaciers of the last ice age. We'd seen them before, these fells of the Yorkshire Dales National Park, on previous family holidays we'd had to Halton Gill, a tiny village, or, I suppose, really more of a hamlet. Halton Gill lies at the head of Littondale, a lonely yet brutally wild and beautiful dale, set deep in the heart of the Yorkshire Pennines.

Horse Head Moor rises in wooded slopes behind Manor Farm, while across the River Skirfare, now brim-full of dark-brown floodwaters straight off the fells, Plover Hill's broad sides curve away to distant Pen-y-Ghent. Further down the dale, on the same, western side of the valley as Pen-y-Ghent, more wooded flanks swell to the flat summit plateau of Darnbrook Fell and Fountains Fell.

These weeks away in the Yorkshire Dales introduced me to a life-long love of nature. This particular week that I'm now thinking back to was mostly spent in a family scrum around the hearth. There were probably five of us kids at that time. Sarah, my younger sister, hadn't been born yet, but was soon to be on the way, and to be honest I say 'probably five of us kids' because I simply can't remember just how many of us were on that particular, wet week away. Our parents, on top of their own offspring, had decided to foster children, and had been doing this for a couple of years. When my mum and dad had started fostering, all of the children they'd looked after in the early years had been babies, but later on kids of all ages stayed with us. So, at any stage during our upbringing there may or may not have been up to two or three other kids in the Uney family, although usually just for a few weeks at a time.

Manor Farm at Halton Gill sits huddled behind a wild rash of a few stone-built cottages and drystone walls, beyond the old chapel. Half of the house was then still lived in by the owners, the Cowans, while the other half they let out for holidays. It was always a great place to go when we were kids. Milk would be collected very early each morning straight from the Friesians in the byre – we could take a container out to this shed in the cold, brittle air of the first minutes of daylight, and Mr Cowan would fill our jug with warm milk straight from the cow, the rest to be collected by tanker later that morning.

We would also get involved in a small way with any odd jobs that needed doing around the farm. I remember Angela, my older sister, and I being asked to catch fledgling pheasants each evening on one holiday. We'd chase them around the yard until they were hemmed in corners, then pick them up and place them carefully in the coop that was their temporary home.

On another occasion we went down to the bridge over the Skirfare with Mrs Cowan to feed the farm ducks. These were special events for a family of town kids such as we were. Picking great armfuls of rhubarb from the kitchen garden was as much a part of our holiday as having a picnic somewhere out on the fell road.

I was probably about eight-years old at the time, and remember two things about that year's holiday that have stayed with me ever since. As I say, it was a particularly wet week. We'd kept out of the rain most of the time, venturing out in the odd dry spells for a stroll along the lane to Foxup, a tiny hamlet a mile or so beyond Halton Gill. Or perhaps we kids had explored up the series of small waterfalls in Halton Gill Beck that lies behind Manor Farm. The rest of the week we were just a family on holiday, in a wonderful, large and rambling farmhouse in the middle of nowhere.

The first thing I recall, and perhaps this was to have a long-lasting effect on me and on the lifestyle I would later choose to follow as an adult, was when my two older brothers, Richard and David, announced that they were off on a fell walk to Hawes. Anybody who is familiar with the Yorkshire Dales might think this was a bit of an odd place to head off to from Halton Gill, but Richard and David were enticed by a signpost on the bend in the road just by the Manor House in which we stayed. It simply said 'Hawes' and pointed blindly up the hill behind the house.

Hawes itself is a lovely market town in the middle of Wensleydale. A glance at the map reveals that there's an awful lot of rough country, and a number of pretty serious ups and downs, in between Halton Gill and Hawes. That was the problem. It was deemed that it was simply too far and too hazardous for me to accompany them. As you can imagine, I was livid. There's a good few years between my two brothers and myself, and my mum and dad obviously thought that I was just too young to go along.

Looking back now, I suspect that Richard and David were actually far too young themselves for such an undertaking, too, and I'm sure that they never got anywhere near Hawes on foot that day. Nevertheless, they came back to the house that night, very late I seem to recall, completely exhausted, but incredibly elated.

Later that same week they were allowed to go off to climb Pen-y-Ghent, and of course I had to stay back with my sisters, Angela and Julie. I'm sure that these two events combined encouraged me to get out into the hills as soon as I was old enough, and no doubt eventually helped to steer me towards a career as a mountain-walking guide and outdoor-pursuits instructor. But more of that later.

The third event of that holiday that has stayed clear in my memory was simple, but again turned out to be life-changing. I think it was the day that Richard and David had gone off to scale Pen-y-Ghent.

I was upstairs in the Manor House, almost certainly sulking, but I can't be sure. I lay on the bed in the enormous room that I shared with my two brothers, reading a book. There was a tap on the window, which I thought very odd, as we were on the top floor of the house. I went over to have a look, but couldn't see anything. As I turned to go back to the bed, there it was again. An obvious tap, repeated a couple of times. As I turned back to the window I just caught sight of a brown blur, as something flew off into the top of a nearby tree.

Intrigued, I pulled up a chair, just back from the window itself, and waited. Within seconds it was back. A small bird, looking very wet and bedraggled. The bird looked almost round, was mid-brown but had the most startling red breast. I'd never knowingly seen anything quite like this before, and I rushed off to tell Julie and Angela what I'd seen.

Obviously, it was a robin, as my dad was able to tell me, and perhaps predictably my two sisters weren't terribly interested in it at all, but that little bird turned around my entire holiday, and possibly my life, too, although I dare say there'd have been another bird pecking at a window sooner or later. But now I was glad I'd not gone up Pen-y-Ghent in the mist and rain. I'd have missed this wonderful little bird if I had.

And here's the thing. Having now seen a robin, and been told by my father what it was, I wanted to know more. What was it doing out there in the rain? Didn't it have a home to go to? Where would it find its food? Was it a boy or a girl robin? Oh and, while we're at it, what's that much bigger, all black bird over there in that bush? And what about the ball-like black-and-white bird that I'd seen bobbing from rock to rock down on the river? What was he, and would he drown if he fell in?

I'd suddenly, completely out of the blue, become interested and, as most boys of that age have a tendency to be, very inquisitive about things, and with me at least, about wildlife in particular. I began keeping a list of birds I'd seen on that wet week in Halton Gill. Some of them I had to look up in a library book I borrowed once we got home, but my list of birds at Halton Gill went something like this:

Robin
Blackbird
Crow
Sparrow
Heron
Pheasant
Wren
Blue tit
Chicken
Pigeon
Dipper

Not massively impressive, I know. But this holiday had really started something. Apart from anything else, I could now recognise eleven different birds (I suppose you could claim that it should only have been ten, and even at that stage in my wildlife-watching career, I'd had to think long and hard about putting that chicken down on my list). The pigeon and crow weren't particularly exciting, but what about the dipper. Here was a little bird that deliberately went into the water. He could cling to the bottom of the river with special claws and trapped air bubbles under his wings so that he could bob back up again whenever he felt like it. Amazing! And I was hooked. I simply wanted to know more, to see more and to see other types of wildlife.

Other family holidays took us to interesting places too. It wasn't that I was completely mad on birds, but I really enjoyed looking out for something new. On our next holiday, to a little wooden chalet at Martham Ferry on the Norfolk Broads, I took along my Bible – *The Observer's Book of Birds*. This enabled me to identify correctly a moorhen, coot, mallard, mute swan, grey heron, reed bunting and, most exciting of all, a kingfisher.

From the chalet, which overlooked the wilder reaches of the River Thurne east of Potter Heigham, we ventured out either on foot, or more often than not, in the little boat that we'd hired for the week. I had no idea back then if there were any of the avian specialities on the Norfolk Broads that I now associate with the region. Today I think of Norfolk and I immediately think of marsh harriers, bearded tits, bitterns and cranes. Back then I suspect these birds were probably very, very rare indeed, but I had plenty to interest me and occupy my time. Canada geese and mute swans seemed to be having chicks all over the place, while moorhens and coots were also ever-present. Grey herons sailed along the river giving off loud, guttural croaks, and kestrels hovered over grassy banks and fields. It was a wonderful time for me, but then most of us are lucky enough to think back to our childhood with fond memories.

I don't quite know why, but looking for birds at that stage seemed to be something I associated with being a holiday pastime. It seems very strange to me now, for although we then lived in Hull, not far at all from the mighty mudflats and swells of the Humber Estuary and just a short drive away from some of eastern England's best nature reserves, such as Spurn Point, Flamborough Head, Bempton Cliffs, Tophill Low and Hornsea Mere, I can't recall a single day spent out birdwatching in that area until I was well into my late teens. No, birdwatching was something I did on holiday. I expect I just didn't think there would be anything of interest in my own backyard.

By the time I came to leave senior school, which in itself had been fairly unpleasant, the only thing I was really sure about was that I wanted to spend my time outdoors, either working with animals, on the land or in any other capacity that would allow me to be free from the tedious factory work that seemed to be the main prospect for school-leavers in Hull in those days. My career adviser had given me surprising advice, considering that I was a pupil of Hull Trinity House School, a school solely interested in getting its pupils into the merchant navy, or so it seemed to me. My grades had been generally good across the board, apart from completely flunking maths, which was a shame as I had a fairly good grasp of the subject but just couldn't get my head straight during the examination. So, when the career adviser, a Mr Rathbone, if I remember correctly, told me, despite my good grades, that the best course of action was either to apply for a job at the British Aerospace factory out at Brough to the west of Hull or to take up an apprenticeship as a builder, I knew immediately that I was very much on my own in making the difficult decision over what to do with my life. That realisation was possibly the most important of my life. Unfortunately, some of my classmates didn't see through Mr Rathbone's plan. I know of at least five of them who are now employed as builders, and two others who still work for British Aerospace.

So, what to do with myself? I don't really know where I got the idea, but I decided to enrol on a course in horticulture at the local agricultural college in the village of Bishop Burton, on the edge of the rolling Yorkshire Wolds. Apart from a solid grounding in the nuances of amenity gardening and propagation, which I loved and took to immediately, the one thing that sticks out from my college days is the first time our group took a walk through the extensive woodlands of the college with two of our tutors, Mike Kinnes and Doug Scott.

We were looking at trees in the late autumn, and Mike and Doug were talking about how to identify them throughout all the seasons. It came to me then, and I can still remember the feeling quite strongly, that what these two tutors were doing with trees was exactly the same as I'd been doing for the last few years with birds and mammals. I was learning about identification. How to tell a willow warbler from a chiffchaff, or a tree sparrow from a house sparrow. Mike and Doug were teaching me how to tell a winter beech from a winter hornbeam by looking at the bark and the shape of the buds, or how to identify an alder by its cones and evergreen leaves. I can't explain how or why, but I immediately warmed to the idea of knowing stuff about plants as well as animals. One seemed to feed off the other, and my thirst for knowledge grew almost overnight. I started to take a real interest in plant identification, not just because I had to do so in order to pass my exams at college, but because I really wanted to know what made that species of clematis, say *Clematis tangutica*, different from another, perhaps a *Clematis vitalba*. Then there was learning how one *Cornus* could be a shrub grown for its brightly coloured stems in winter, while another *Cornus* could be a small tree grown for its wonderfully variegated leaves in the summer.

This passed on to my interest in wildlife, and now I stopped thinking in terms of birdwatching as being a holiday pursuit and started coming to the realisation that this was something I was doing all the time.

In his fabulous and very sensible book *How to be a Bad Birdwatcher*, Simon Barnes makes a very good point about learning about birds. He says that he doesn't go out specifically birdwatching, he simply is birdwatching all of the time. When I read his book and came across that passage, I knew exactly what he meant. I've been doing the same thing ever since I learnt at college how to really look at the details of a thing, be it a herbaceous perennial in a walled-garden border, a dragonfly on a summer pond or a wader freshly arrived from the Arctic.

With this realisation came the desire to know more about the wild world that seemed to surround me. Wherever I went I came across it. Wildlife was, and still is, despite the worst intentions of humans, everywhere.

Holderness House is a large private residential home for refined ladies in east Hull. Working in the grounds of this stately pile as the Assistant Head Gardener gave me the opportunity to watch wildlife every day. By that, I don't mean I took my binoculars to work with me and sat there looking for birds. I mean I was surrounded by wildlife throughout the year – through the changing seasons.

Summer brought spotted flycatchers to the area around our compost bins. There was an endless supply of food here for them, and I could stand quite close and watch these little speckled jobs take off from a perch on a nearby bough or sometimes on the wooden sides of the compost bins themselves. They'd launch after a passing insect, snatch it out of the air, then nine times out of ten, would return to the same branch to eat their catch.

There were foxes that burrowed into a bank of earth upon which the house itself sat, and most evenings you could sit with your back to the huge hornbeam tree that towered over the lawn and watch the foxes emerge from their den. Winter brought large flocks of tits and finches, plus lots of fieldfares and redwings most years, and I kept note of all the species that came and went through the seasons.

All this time I'd also begun exploring further afield. Wild coasts, moorlands and mountains in particular fascinated me, and still do to this day. And most weekends would find me off to one or other of the valleys of the Lake District where I'd pitch my tent and use that as a base from which to explore. I soon got to know Lakeland very well, particularly the fells around Borrowdale, Wasdale, Langdale and Patterdale, and this naturally led on to a desire to explore Wales and Scotland.

Another of those life-changing events came when Gore-Tex, the makers of waterproof materials for outdoor-pursuit enthusiasts, sponsored me to take part in a Mountain Leader Training Course at the National Mountain Centre, Glenmore Lodge, in the Cairngorms. Although I was still working as a gardener at Holderness House, this gave me the idea that I could perhaps have a career change and turn instead to outdoor pursuits. I would eventually do this, but not for a number of years, although I would indeed soon have a change of career.

My love of the outdoors spurred me to begin writing short features on wildlife, the environment and walking. I sent many of these off to the various magazines that specialised in these subjects, and within months I had had a few of my features published in *TGO* magazine. The thrill of seeing my first piece in print, a slightly odd feature about a double crossing of the North York Moors National Park on foot, following the ancient route, the Lyke Wake Walk, has stayed with me to this day.

Soon, my local newspaper, the *Hull Daily Mail* showed an interest in my putting together a weekly column covering walks somewhere in East Yorkshire, either in the Yorkshire Wolds or on the Holderness Plain, and slowly my career changed itself.

I took on more and more writing commissions, and by that time, I knew that this was something I had to immerse myself in fully. I felt I needed something meatier to get my teeth into, and so decided to write a book about the mountains of Wales. So that I had to commit to my new project 100 per cent, rather than trying to do this while also keeping my gardening job, I decided that the best way to get to know all of the mountain ranges of Wales would be to plan a continuous walk over all of them. This would take two months and would necessitate handing in my notice at Holderness House. My life as a writer had begun.

My Welsh walk was a tremendous success, more so than the book which followed. But at least I now had a new career path, and a completely new way of life. I took on work with the East Riding of Yorkshire County Council Adult Education Service as a tutor, organising a programme of walks for them, and later a series of wildlife-watching courses too. These were great fun and led to my second book being published, a book of walks in East Yorkshire. This also helped me to develop an even greater knowledge of the county, as I had to try each week to come up with a new location to take a largish group of retirees, each of whom had spent the best part of their lives exploring Yorkshire. Imagination was called for, and it seemed that I had plenty of this, to the extent that I was soon running five separate classes for three different Adult Education Centres across the county, with up to forty people enrolling for each class.

As I travelled out and about in East Yorkshire I slowly built up in my mind a picture of the county throughout the seasons. I had a pretty good all-round knowledge of the area, and could often pick the best location to go to see wildlife with my groups. We started doing bird counts, and on some days out as a group we'd see getting on for 100 species, and this started my, possibly overactive, brain thinking. I reasoned that there probably weren't too many people in the county with such a broad knowledge of wildlife. True, there were many people with a deeper understanding of say, bird migration, deer populations, badger haunts, beetle species or whatever, but as an overall wildlife enthusiast, I fancied myself as being up there with the best of them. I began research for a guidebook on where to watch wildlife in East Yorkshire, a weighty tome which is complete, but sadly unpublished and sitting in a cardboard box in my loft. I wanted to spend as much time as possible out in the field watching wildlife – not just birds, but all wildlife. To accompany me on my field trips I found the most obvious companion, though one who I didn't immediately recognise as being at all interested in wildlife – my older brother, Dave.

We spent hundreds of hours out exploring the reserves of East Yorkshire together. From the muddy fields of Sunk Island and Cherry Cobb Sands to the reedbeds of Saltmarsh Delph and Welton Waters, we combed every corner of our county. This sudden surge of interest from both of us, combined with my love of the hillier parts of the country, led to Dave and I making plans for trips to Scotland, home of what is amusingly known among the wildlife tourism trade as 'charismatic megafauna'. Think big and beautiful and you've got the idea! We wanted to see red deer, pine martens, Scottish wildcats, golden eagles, ospreys, crested tits, crossbills, capercaillies, minke whales, bottlenose dolphins, and much more besides.

I well remember our first trip away with wildlife photography as our aim. Dave and I were staying at West Laroch on the north side of the Ballachulish Bridge on Loch Leven. We'd had a couple of days over in Moidart and Sunart, beautiful and wild regions to the west of Loch Linnhe, and had managed to get shots of red deer in the hills, a few eiders on the shores of Loch Sunart and the odd distant grey seal. However, we both felt that we could do a lot better with red deer than we thought we might have already achieved. This was in the days before we both turned to digital photography. We were both shooting transparency film and wouldn't know the results of our efforts until we had the films developed later. Unfortunately, we were both very green back then, both in terms of our understanding of 'wild' deer behaviour and also photographically.

We'd started the day by running out of petrol before we even got out of the car park at the B&B. I knew that there was a petrol station in Glencoe village a short walk back along the road, so we got the spare can out of the car, and with me grumbling about the stupidity of my older brother (we were in his car), we set off on foot.

One positive decision that morning had been to take our cameras. Within a few hundred yards we'd snapped a buzzard sitting in typical pose atop a telegraph post, as well as a grey heron lazily flapping along the lochside, which runs parallel to the road throughout this stretch of Glencoe.

As we neared the road junction at the petrol station, one of us spotted a vague movement down on the shore. There's a bit of saltmarsh here, scarred by run-off channels, and at first all we could see through our binoculars was a scum-covered shore and four oystercatchers picking among the pebbles. Then something brown scurried between channels and vanished again. We could now see a group of mallards floating into view, and for a while we convinced ourselves that these were probably what had caught our eye. I could tell that Dave wasn't really satisfied with this explanation, though, and he was right of course. Mallards tend not to scurry particularly well! We stood on the roadside for a good 20 minutes or more, and still couldn't see anything other than mallards – even the oystercatchers had flown off in the direction of the opposite shore.

Then, just as we were about to lose heart, we both saw it again at the same time. A sleek, brown body and whiskery face pushed easily through the water, sliding a long tail behind. Our first wild otter was just 40 yards away from us beside one of the busiest roads in the Scottish Highlands. As we watched in complete, bewildered delight, he flicked seaweed into the air then dived deep, coming up in mid-channel with a great green pelt of shining wrack on his head. Through the mass of sparkling kelp, this large dog otter looked at me for a couple of seconds, straight down the twin lenses of my binoculars. Then a quick flick of his tail and in an instant he was gone. Neither of us had thought to try for a photograph. We'd been far too busy enjoying our first otter, and the thought hadn't even crossed our minds. Some great wildlife photographers we were destined to become!

Still, this had obviously cheered us both up, and Dave was quick to point out (in fact, he still mentions it from time to time!) that had he filled up with petrol the night before we would never have seen that otter. So, spurred on by our success as wildlife spotters we decided to spend the day trying for more red deer photos.

Glen Etive is a great trench that cuts down through the hills from the raised plateau of Rannoch Moor. To the east, the rough chain of hills rises to the high summits of the Black Mount, while westwards even greater mountains form the southern boundary to Glen Coe itself. The Etive is a great river, in places forcing a rough and tumbling gorge through the stunning Highland scenery, and here in the valley bottom there are often big herds of red deer.

Where the A82 spews out onto the open vastness of Rannoch Moor, squeezing between the rocky bastions of Buachaille Etive Mor on the right and the rounded curves of Beinn a' Chrulaiste on the left, the whole expanse of the moor stretches for miles eastwards. There's the Kings House Hotel, nestled down by the River Etive, then nothing but wonderful, barren moorland until the fine cone of Schiehallion cuts the sky far out in the distance.

Here a little dead-end road winds down the valley, keeping close to the river throughout, simply because there's not much space in the glen bottom for both. We crossed the bridge where the River Coupall comes in from the other side of Buachaille Etive Mor – the big shepherd of Etive. There, on the flanks of this great mountain, but quite a way uphill, we spotted a small herd of red deer.

Dave pulled in and we scanned the slopes with binoculars, silently wondering how easy it would be to stalk these beasts with the cameras. Fortunately, before we could egg each other on too much, I saw another group further down the glen, and much closer to the road.

I'd read somewhere that deer, as with many wild animals, don't seem to mind cars, so long as you drive carefully and slowly up to them, avoiding sudden movement, but once you get out they'll see the form of a human instead of a box on wheels, and will leg it uphill. You can use your car as a mobile hide, so Dave glided gently down the glen until we were just across from 15 fine stags. This really was turning into a superb day – we'd already photographed a buzzard, grey herons, oystercatchers and seen an otter, and here we were just 200 yards from a herd of red deer stags.

We took a couple of dozen shots each, and then, perhaps inevitably, Dave asked, 'Do you think we could get any closer?'

'Not sure. We'd have to stalk them and try to use what cover we can.'

We naively seemed to think that the deer hadn't seen or heard us at this point, which of course they had, so we opened the car doors as quietly as we could, slid out and pushed them closed. Then, walking ponderously in a kind of crouched shuffle, we made our way through the bracken and bog myrtle towards the deer. As we got closer, I suspected that the deer might just be on to us, so we got down on hands and knees and began to crawl. I'd read somewhere that no animal likes to be approached directly, so our approach became a wild series of long zigzags. Over boulders, through peat and bracken, and across a small burn at one point, we Commando-crawled towards the unsuspecting deer.

Half an hour later and we'd made good progress, so good in fact that we were now within 10 feet of one of the stags. We lay there on the heathery slope, our clothes blackened from sliding through peat and wet to the skin from crawling through the burn, but at least we had been successful. We glanced across at each other.

'Let's hope the camera shutters aren't too loud,' I murmured to Dave, for at this stage I was, stupidly, still convinced that the deer didn't know that we were there. I took a few photographs, actually having to zoom out with my 300 mm lens, as I was just too close to get the whole deer in the frame.

Looking at these photos now, with the deer glaring back at me straight down the lens, I cringe at how naive we had been. Obviously the deer knew we were there, and probably had done since we first stopped the car further up the road to watch the other herd higher up the mountain.

Once we'd each taken all the photographs we needed, we were able to slowly stand and approach even closer to the deer. I looked across at Dave, who was covered in muck and grime, then down at my clothes, which were the same. We beamed broadly at each other and felt that we'd at last made it as wildlife photographers.

Further down the glen, there were huge herds of deer in the woods around Dalness, and at the foot of the glen, just as the road comes to an end at the small public car park at Gualachulain, we strolled down to the shore of Loch Etive, spotting a couple of red-breasted mergansers out on the water.

Overhead, a small skein of geese flew low along the loch, using the long curves as a guide. These were almost certainly winter visitors from Greenland, a small group of barnacle geese heading down to the sea at Loch Creran.

3

Settling in Scotland

Scotland gets under your skin. By the summer of 2002, it had certainly got under mine. I was working full time as a writer and photographer, and deliberately targeted magazine and newspaper features at anyone who would pay for me to cover stories on the Highlands and Islands.

It was yet another grey and overcast, but dry, day. I drove over the broad, sparse heather moors of Lochindorb, stopping to watch a pair of short-eared owls hunting for voles over a large section of last season's muir-burn. I was heading for Inverness Airport from the direction of Boat of Garten in the Cairngorms where I'd been photographing red squirrels feeding in the tops of pine trees at the RSPB reserve at Loch Garten. The plan had been to while away a few days in the remnants of the ancient Caledonian pine forest there, prior to flying north to meet a group of journalists on Orkney. All had gone very well up to that point, and during my short stay in the Cairngorms, I'd also tracked and photographed a roe deer doe through the luxuriant moss and blaeberry growth, tangled beneath the splendid canopy of dark Caledonian pines, and had photographed Slavonian grebes over at the Loch Ruthven RSPB Reserve west of the A9.

Orkney had fascinated me for a long time. Perhaps not too surprisingly, it was the birdlife of the islands that was the draw, more so than the archaeological remains, although obviously I was keen to see those too. I'd been to the Shetland Isles on a press trip the year before and expected Orkney to be much the same. This time, the trip was to be split into two halves, with the first few days being spent exploring Orkney. Then we'd transfer to Shetland, so we'd get the chance to compare the two island groups side by side, as it were.

The flight from Inverness to Kirkwall was uneventful, apart from opening up impressive views of the whole east coast of Scotland from the Moray Firth upwards. The tiny plane bounced roughly along the runway at Kirkwall Airport and taxied to a halt in front of the squat, grey terminal building. Over on some rough, grassy ground, east of the main runway, I could see movement. A pale, long-winged bird caught my eye. I watched it as it quartered the ground, passing in long runs back and forth over the wasteland. Twice it seemed to stall almost in the air, and then continued hunting in graceful sweeps. Five minutes on Orcadian soil, and I was watching a male hen harrier, even before I'd stepped from the plane.

The Scottish Tourist Board, or at least their walking holiday promotions division, Walking Wild, had arranged the trip for us, a group of half a dozen or so freelance journalists from around the country. Between us we were working for a broad range of publications, and the group included the editor of a new overseas walking magazine, a freelance writer working for *Family Circle*, a BBC photographer, a freelance journalist writing various travel features for Scottish newspapers, a chief sub-editor from a woman's health and fitness magazine, and myself. Walking Wild had sent along a representative, an affable chap called Colin, who was to be our guide for the week.

Colin and Felicity, the freelance from the Scottish papers, were on my flight, but of course I hadn't known this until Colin introduced himself as we entered the airport buildings. We transferred to the hotel in Kirkwall and met the rest of the group just before dinner.

I suppose I really should say that my attention was distracted entirely by Olivia, the chief sub-editor from *Shape*, the woman's health magazine. Sadly, I honestly can't claim that that's what happened, romantic though that would be, and I know that looking back now she can't really remember me being there that first evening either. Strange, since we got on so well during the rest of the trip, and within months of our returning home I'd upped-sticks and left my homeland of East Yorkshire to move in with Olivia in a large flat in Clapton, a sprawling nonsense of grimy town houses sandwiched between Hackney and Stoke Newington in north-east London. It must have been love!

Orkney was wonderful; Shetland, even better, and within a couple of months of my moving down to London, Olivia and I talked about how much we missed the wildness of these places, the wildlife there and how free we both felt when we were in Scotland. I guess it was inevitable, but Clapton drove us mad. I wanted open spaces, and found it difficult to escape the confines of London, and Olivia had left a flat in Hampstead and missed the openness and familiar beauty of the Heath. She'd also had enough of working on *Shape* and suspected that things were not going well at higher managerial levels within the magazine, and so we talked of moving out of London altogether.

Initially we moved sideways, to Chingford on the edge of Epping Forest, and then as things got worse at work for Olivia, the draw of Scotland grew stronger and I decided to talk to the Scottish Youth Hostel Association about taking on the management of a hostel in the Highlands. This, of course, would have been a completely new change of direction for both of us, and we were excited by the prospect of moving to the Highlands.

Plans came together slowly. The SYHA asked if we could move to Strathpeffer, a wonderful old Victorian spa town near Beauly, as they had an old rambling building there that they were trying to sell and basically wanted someone to caretake for them. This arrangement suited us fine. We struck a deal which I felt definitely leaned in our favour. We would live in this enormous house set above the town, rent-free, and the SYHA would pay a small wage for me to look after the place until they found a buyer. Meanwhile, Olivia got in touch with Jim Love, the editor of *The Inverness Courier*, to see if they could offer her any freelance sub-editing work.

We drove north from Chingford in a large white van, heavily laden with most of our possessions. The Victorian Highland town of Strathpeffer cowered beneath dank storm clouds as we arrived at dusk the following day. Elsick House lies at the far end of the main street, huddled on two sides by conifer trees, with an old orchard on a third, and the road itself on the fourth. Its cold towers and austere façade seemed to glower threateningly down at the two townies who parked outside on the driveway. We turned the key in the lock and pushed open the door, sweeping a huge pile of mail aside as we stepped gingerly into the porch of our new home. It was freezing inside – colder than it had been out. The lights didn't work, and we couldn't remember where the torch had been packed. As one does, we muddled through such trying times.

We left the van full for the night, found the electrical cupboard and flipped the switches. Our new home was revealed. A warming fire in the hearth, a take-away Indian meal from Dingwall just down the road and a bottle of French wine, and things began to feel not so bad after all.

Life at Elsick House was fun, but also very trying. We were still very much getting to know each other. Olivia was struggling to be enthused by a life of editing tedious reports and features at *The Inverness Courier*, and I was trying to establish a series of skills courses that I aimed to run for hillwalkers. Writing work was in short supply, as was photography, but we scrimped and mostly got by.

Sitting at my desk one morning, just a couple of days after we'd moved in, I happened to glance out of the window to the garden overlooking the town. Great conifer trees studded the lawn, and a smudge of dark rhododendrons skulked in the far corner. Between the tops of the trees I caught an all-too-brief glimpse of a large bird, definitely a raptor, and I wasn't sure but I thought I'd seen a forked tail.

I grabbed a pair of binoculars and rushed outside onto the lawn. Scanning through the dense canopy of pine needles was difficult, but I knew that the bird had been flying from out of the woods and in the direction of the road, so I dashed off in that direction, and there it was. A magnificent red kite. The boggy, moorland bumps of Mid Wales were then the only place I'd ever seen these wonderful carrion-eating birds of prey before, but I knew that there had been reintroduction schemes in various parts of the country by the RSPB. This bird must have been from the nearby Black Isle relocation.

He swung about on the breeze, using his forked tail as a rudder, and then alighted in the top branches of an old oak tree way out over the other side of the town.

Soon after my red kite sighting we were having a lazy Sunday morning in bed reading the papers. It was Olivia this time that caught a glimpse of the obvious outline of the kite, floating by our bedroom window. We leapt out of bed and sprang to the window from where the kite could just be seen flying eastwards towards the woods that covered the flanks of Knockfarrel, a heather and bracken covered ridge rising in rocky folds above the house. We soon lost sight of him, but noticed a couple of smaller birds in the crumbling apple trees of the old orchard. I went to get the binoculars while Olivia kept her eyes on the birds as they flitted about. When I returned, a couple of bullfinches filled our view, picking delicately at the buds of the fruit trees as the warmth of the spring day enticed them to open.

The lounge in the staff quarters of the hostel benefited greatly by having a lovely window seat with a three-quarters of a circle curved glass window. We often sat there of an evening, reading, listening to music, and while there was still some spring light left in the sky, watching the birds that came to the feeders that we'd hung from one of the apple trees right outside the window.

These were usually a bit of a mixed batch of chaffinches, greenfinches and siskins, along with blue, great and coal tits, but for a week or two during the latter part of the winter and early spring, we had three bramblings feeding there along with the other birds.

Walks along the Knockfarrel ridge were a nice way to spend a few hours. There are the sad remains of a vitrified fort at the eastern end, almost overlooking Dingwall, while from anywhere along the ridge you look northwards to the bold, elongated arms of Ben Wyvis, sloping down to the River Peffery. Southwards the views extended over the colourful farmlands of the River Ord to the small, outlying peaks of the Glen Affric chain. We regularly spotted red kites floating along with the thermals that rose from the hill, and common buzzards were usually in the skies here too.

The spring that year was stunning. The fields and farms were bathed in warm, golden light for weeks at a time, and wildlife seemed to flourish. We did too.

Olivia was settling in a little better at *The Inverness Courier*. They seemed to appreciate having her there, and apart from the weekly chore of having to sub-edit the shinty results, a sport the likes of which Olivia had never even heard of just a few weeks before, and the Gaelic pages, which she couldn't read (nor incidentally, could anyone else at the paper, it seemed), she was feeling pretty good about things.

I had taken on more writing work and had managed to get off the ground a handful of navigation courses aimed at hillwalkers. I ran these courses straight from home, taking clients up through the woods either on Knockfarrel, or via Loch Kinellen down towards the Rogie Falls on the Blackwater. These courses were great fun and seemed to be as much a social event as a serious skills-based course, but that was absolutely fine by me. I'd start off by teaching the very basics of map and compass work, and usually found that most of my clients already had the rudimentary skills, such as reading grid references and understanding about map scales and signs. We would then look at measuring distances on the map, and then on the ground by counting the amount of double steps each individual took to walk 100 metres. It seemed that no matter how much I stressed the importance of walking in as normal a manner as possible when doing this, every day I'd get at least one person who would shuffle along, then at the end of 100 metres announce that they'd taken 154 double steps (bearing in mind that most people take somewhere in between 55 and 75 over 100 metres). Either that or there'd be some sort of Monty Python Ministry of Funny Walks going on, and then they'd say that their tally had been 32 double steps, or some such mad figure. Once these skills had been mastered correctly, we'd then look at taking and following compass bearings, often to path junctions or streams or some such, but sometimes I'd ask them to go to a non-existent point on the map, like the letter 'o' in the word Knockfarrel, or the point where two grid lines cross. All good fun, and it certainly got me out into the local woods and hills.

One day I'd been out walking with a group in the woods around the village of Contin. I got home just as darkness was creeping in, removed my walking boots in the porch, put the kettle on and went to check for telephone messages. There was one from the SYHA headquarters in Stirling, saying that they'd found a buyer for Elsick House and could I call them back as soon as possible. It seemed that we were going to be made homeless, and, unfortunately for us, the sale had progressed very quickly, which gave us just a few days to find somewhere else to live.

Modern flats in Inverness seemed tiny by comparison to Elsick House. We viewed a few that were quite expensive to rent, but just within our budget, but found it hard to be enthusiastic about trying to fit all of our belongings into a bijou one-up and two-down. In desperation we'd trudged around all of the estate agents we could find and were sitting in the Blackfriars pub in Inverness having a pint of real ale when I spotted an advert in *The Inverness Courier*.

It read: 'Estate Cottage to let between Inverness and Ullapool' and gave a telephone number for one of the few lettings agents we hadn't yet tried. Olivia got on the phone immediately, and within 20 minutes we were sitting in the upstairs offices of the agents in Inverness arranging a viewing.

The only problem was that we'd almost decided that we really wanted to be living back in the town. Strathpeffer felt far too countrified for this couple of townies, albeit townies who loved the countryside, hence our trawling around the streets of Inverness. This was clearly going to be a very rural property, but we thought it might just be worth a look.

The following Saturday morning we drove the few miles down the road from Strathpeffer to Garve, clattered over the railway via the level crossing, and turned sharp right into the village. We'd been given directions to Crannach by the factor, a young woman called Sue, and followed them over the metal bridge over the Blackwater, down a long straight driveway to the foot of Little Wyvis, then turned into the private driveway of the house. An old coach house with double doors and a stable block faced the car park, and Sue popped her head round the corner from the garden to greet us. Before we'd even got out of the car we'd both fallen completely head over heals in love with the place.

We signed the papers and moved in a couple of days later.

Garve set us deep in the heart of the Ross-shire Highlands. Crannach is set well out of the village in what is known as Strathgarve, on the east side of the valley away from the main road, the railway and the village itself. We soon settled in and got on with having a quiet life.

Wildlife surrounded us in everything we did and everywhere we went. On occasions it would even welcome itself into our cottage.

One night shortly after we'd moved in I heard Olivia getting out of bed in the middle of the night. I turned over, sleepy and confused in the darkness.

'What's the matter, Livi?' I asked.

'There's something moving around in here,' she answered.

'What, a mouse or something?'

'Don't know. I think it's got wings!'

I got out of bed and put the light on. Nothing at all. We often slept with the bedroom door and the windows open, so I went out onto the landing to investigate, and, switching on the landing light, I met a pipistrelle bat flying up the stairs towards me. This cute little bundle of fur must have come in through the open window and was now looking for the way out. He flew into our spare room and we followed him in and closed the door behind us. I went over to open the windows and we sat and watched as the tiny bat covered all areas of the small room, mapping the dimensions of the small rectangular space in his mind, and no doubt marking objects such as the wardrobe and desk. We watched him for 10 minutes or so, as he made a few passes near the open window. He then flew to the far end of the room, turned and took a direct line out into the open air. We closed the windows and went back to bed, happy to have shared a few minutes of our night-time with a bat.

There is a little lane behind the stable block at Crannach that leads along the length of the strath. To the south it leads to Loch Garve, a beautiful stretch of water with common sandpipers and ospreys in the summer, and divers and mergansers in the winter. Beautiful to look at, but unfortunately scarred along its shores by huge dumps of rubbish. Masses of part-buried plastic sheeting, old tyres, bedspreads, oil drums and loads of other clutter ruin this once stunning place. Most of this detritus must have been there for some time, as slowly it is being covered by moss and creeping grasses, but we felt that the wind had been taken out of our sails when we first walked along the shores of the loch and saw mile after mile of this garbage. We began clearing it up, but then I'm ashamed to say that we just gave up. There was, and probably still is, just far too much of it.

The road runs in the other direction to an old bridge. This was constructed by Major Caulfield – successor to the famous General Wade – in 1752 as part of a military road from Contin to Poolewe, to cross the Blackwater. Here new plantations of Scots pines clad the heathery lower slopes of the two hills that rose above. Ben Wyvis throws down its flanks to the gurgling rush of the Blackwater's surge, while immediately above the bridge the gentler flanks of Little Wyvis are also a worthy walk for any hillwalker. We ventured onto these tops a number of times, but more often than not, it would be the woods that we'd enjoy exploring more.

The river itself is magnificent. It drains the vastness of Loch Vaich in Easter Ross, and here below Wyvis it squeezes spectacularly through great shelving slabs of dark rock. There are paths on either side of the river, heading upstream from the bridge at Little Garve, and we'd often do a circuit up to Silverbridge, another military construction, a mile or so in both directions.

The Blackwater River is very well named. The peat dragged down from the higher moors stains it to a very dark, porter colour, and salmon leap up the numerous falls to their spawning grounds on the gravel beds further upstream.

We watched grey wagtails feeding their chicks here in the summer, and common sandpipers bobbing on rounded stones in the riverbed. Crested tits forage in the pine trees, some of which looked very old and gnarly, and crossbills flit by in huge flocks in the spring.

We had a number of bird feeders in the garden, and Sue asked us if we'd keep records of everything we saw there. This started out by being fairly straightforward,

26

then became more and more exciting as I realised just how wonderful a habitat we occupied.

In addition to the birds on the feeders, which included all the usual sparrows, tits and finches, there were also lots of more unusual passerines, such as redpolls, crossbills, crested tits, siskins, yellowhammers, reed buntings and blackcaps. Ospreys often flew by over the meadows on their way between Loch Garve and Loch Vaich, and hen harriers and red kites were also occasionally seen quartering the ground. Buzzards were everywhere, but I remember on at least one occasion scanning the ridge on the opposite side of the strath and catching a golden eagle hunting boldly into the wind.

'You'll never guess what's just been in our house,' Olivia greeted me one day as I arrived home from a walk on Little Wyvis. She'd arrived home from work in Inverness and had left the front door wide open as she went through to the kitchen to unpack a load of shopping. Fifteen minutes later she'd finished stocking the shelves, made herself a cup of tea, and decided to take it out into the garden. As she walked up the corridor that led from the front door to the kitchen, she spotted a bird hopping along the passageway. She put her cup on the sideboard and bent down to see a female siskin looking brightly up at her.

She tried to coax it towards the door, but the little thing just hopped about. The only thing she could think to do was try to catch it, but didn't think that this was going to be at all easy. How wrong she was. The tiny finch just sat there and let her pick it up. She was delighted at the little bundle of feathers, so light and fragile did it seem. She carried it to the door and placed it on the grass underneath the feeders. Within minutes it had flown away and joined the rest of the small flock that lived in the alder trees at the bottom of the garden. We could only assume that it had become disorientated after flying through the open door.

Work took an interesting turn for me while we were at Garve. I decided to try to put my mountain leader qualifications to some good use, and so spent an afternoon writing up my CV. An internet search revealed a dozen or more walking holiday companies that I thought might be worth trying for some freelance work, so I printed off a load of copies of my CV and popped them in the post.

Within days I'd had a call from Paul Milligan who then owned Lomond Walking Holidays. I travelled down to his home near Stirling for a chat. I sat in his living room amid piles of baby clothes and other new-parent paraphernalia while his wife brought tea and biscuits, her delightful new baby held tightly in her arms. By the end of the day I had been offered a couple of weeks' work as a guide with the company.

The first of these weeks was for a group of retirees who wanted to explore the area north of Ullapool, from a base at Inchnadamph at the heart of Assynt. We had a great time, and despite the advanced age of most of the people in the group, they managed to climb a good few mountains and were cheerful and chatty the whole week.

The second trip I did for Paul Milligan was to Knoydart, an area that at that time I didn't know that well at all. The trip was for a very mixed group and the weather was a real boiler. In the space of a week we polished off all of the Munros and Corbetts on the peninsula and really got to see the better side of this remote place.

More work dripped in from other companies. I worked with Frazer Fotheringham from Ullapool, and Beryl Tudhope, a good friend of mine from Herefordshire, with a large group from the Faroe Islands who were on a grand tour of the Highlands. During the long week with the Faroese we led them on some superb walks in Glen Affric, the Cairngorms and Assynt, which were all wonderful, but the most memorable thing about that particular trip was the daily ritual of singing the Faroese national anthem at the start of each walk. Each day we'd drive the group in a couple of minibuses to the start point of the walk. We would lace up our boots, pull on our rucksacks and then, just as we were ready to set off, the Faroese would start singing a very slow, very solemn, dirge-like anthem. We guides lost track of the seemingly endless verses, as they all sounded pretty much the same to us, but each time we thought they'd finished and prepared to go, they'd start up again on the next verse. This usually took up a good 20 minutes or so, but they seemed so happy afterwards that it seemed churlish to say anything to them about it.

There's a great little pub on the outskirts of Inverness. The Clachnaharry is a true drinker's haven, and we often popped by for a pint of real ale on the way home from a shopping trip or if we'd been down to the Cairngorms for a walk.

One afternoon we were sitting in the snug wood-panelled bar with a pint of Red Kite each when Olivia looked up from the newspaper she was reading.

'Have you seen this?' she asked. 'You should send them your CV.'

I read the piece and was immediately impressed by the blurb which the *Press and Journal* had printed about a new company that was organising wilderness walking holidays in the Highlands.

Wilderness Scotland was set up by Neil Birnie and Paul Easto, two young professional men who lived in Edinburgh, and Neil's dad, Gordon, who lived in Rafford in Morayshire.

I first met Neil in a café at the Kyle of Lochalsh one wet and horrible day a month or so later. We chatted about their company ethos, which seemed to match my own ideas about running walking holidays, and there and then Neil offered me a job as a freelance guide. That meeting led to an exciting few years of new adventures.

Within weeks I was meeting groups most Saturday mornings and taking them off for the week to the far corners of the Highlands. The Cairngorms, Assynt, Wester Ross, Knoydart and the Outer Hebrides all became regular haunts, and the job gave me the chance to meet some great people, and hopefully to give them an enjoyable and informative holiday in the Highlands and Islands.

These Wilderness Scotland trips also gave me a great opportunity to get to know more about the wildlife of these wild places. Each week away seemed to be just as much a holiday for me as it was for the clients. I got to know likely places in Knoydart, Harris and Lewis for spotting golden eagles, or on Canna, Mull and Eigg for white-tailed eagles. Red deer were commonplace, and shorebirds featured heavily on all of the trips. Otters were still as elusive as ever, but I managed to show my groups individuals on trips every few weeks or so. And bear in mind that these were walking holidays, not wildlife holidays.

However, I like to think that I still make my trips with Wilderness Scotland my own, although I know that the other guides have their own particular ways of running a holiday and have their own interests to pass on to the clients.

4

From source to sea

We hadn't even reached the hide when the skein came low over our heads in a wildly cackling, black-and-white squadron, 3,000 strong. And when I say low, I mean low! Dipping wings to each side in order to lose height, web-footed feet splayed out front to act as brakes, the barnacle geese landed among the crusty winter stubbles just 20 yards from where we stood, each of us mesmerised and breathless. Yet at Mersehead RSPB Reserve on the Scottish side of the Solway Firth, this kind of thing happens all the time during the winter. Around 23,000 of these birds make their end-of-breeding-season flight from Svalbard in the Arctic to the Solway Firth in Britain for the winter, so this skein was actually only a very small percentage of the total number that could have swooped over us right then.

Down on the estuary other wildfowl were much in evidence. Huge flotillas of wigeon and pintail dabbled off shore, while a flock of 100 or so scaup flew past in a humbug-coloured huddle and landed on the muddy levels of the Firth. This elegant sea duck is a speciality of the inner waters of the Solway Firth – counts in recent years of 2,500 birds represent about 23 per cent of the British population, making the Firth one of its most important overwintering grounds.

Across the Firth the mighty hills of the Skiddaw Fells of Lakeland formed a dark-blue smudge beneath grey nimbus clouds, adding another dimension to the atmosphere of the scene.

The Solway Firth is Britain's third largest area of continuous intertidal habitat, a fact that makes it perfectly suitable for the hundreds of thousands of wintering wildfowl and waders that arrive there each autumn. The brown waters flow westwards between Dumfries and Galloway in Scotland and Cumbria in England and form one of the finest winter birdwatching destinations in Britain, simply because if large flocks of Arctic ducks, geese, swans or waders happen to be your thing, this is where the vast majority of them will be during the cold, dark months. Most of Europe's wildfowl and wader species breed high in the Arctic Circle, nesting and feeding on the ground among low vegetation. Once the snows arrive in these northern climes the birds' food supply becomes buried beneath the frozen wastes, and so a steady migration southwards occurs, bringing huge numbers of birds to the relatively balmy coastal waters of Britain. Here food is plentiful in the form of winter crops, stubble fields and saltmarsh vegetation, and this is why the Solway Firth is such an important site for these birds in winter.

The Scottish side of the Firth is a large mosaic of fields, woods, nature reserves and extensive coastal sites, offering a broad range of habitats to tempt all kinds of birds, whereas the Cumbrian side of the estuary is designated as an Area of Outstanding Natural Beauty. The Solway Coast AONB was designated in 1964 and stretches from Rockcliffe Marsh near Carlisle in the east to Maryport in the west. The basis of this designation is to conserve and enhance the natural beauty of the whole area.

The Solway Coast in its present form has been part of the landscape for at least 10,000 years – ever since the retreat of the vast ice sheet that covered this part of the country during the last ice age. Over these past 10,000 years, humans have settled in the area and, with stone axe and adze, saws, ploughs and tractors, have cleared woodlands, withies and marsh, creating this impressive range of habitats. Having said that, some of the lands around the Solway are still relatively unspoilt, but others have been modified and cleared almost to the point of destruction. The Romans, Vikings, the Border Reivers and eventually modern man have shaped the Solway Coast into what it is today.

The Solway begins its life in two areas, both of them wild upland regions cutting through the backbone of Britain.

Just a few yards west of the summit of Hugh Seat stands a stone pillar. High on this bleak Pennine moor, 2,260 feet higher than the Solway, and many a rough mile away, Lady's Pillar was erected in 1664 by Lady Anne Clifford in memory of Sir Hugh Morville. Hugh Seat itself is not particularly exciting but has the distinction of having three of northern England's mightiest rivers rising about its summit plateau. The Ure and Swale wallow eventually eastwards out into the Humber Estuary, but a short moorland walk away to the north from their sources you'll find Eden Springs. The streams here are sluggish at first and seem to have to push a way through the peaty morass in order to make any headway. Red Gill is the name given to the tiny stream that flows from Eden Springs, and this little waterway changes in name numerous times as it gains in girth and weight, feeling gravity's pull on its long journey downhill to the Solway Firth.

It flounders across Black Fell Moss, through a landscape seemingly devoid of life, but full of names redolent of bleakness and wildness. Names like Burnt Crag, Scarth of Scaiths, Black Paddock and Black Gutter. The infant Eden splutters across these untamed moors, passing places with names such as Sour Hill, Black

Hill and Far Capple Mere, then merrily throws itself off a brief cliff at Hell Gill Bridge. Well, with that kind of upbringing, who could blame it?

Just 500 yards away to the south lies Ure Crook – a big bend in the infant River Ure. For raindrops falling on these moors between the two it's a very close call as to whether they'll find the sea to the east or to the west.

A short hop down from Hell Gill Bridge, twisting a course through the rough grasslands of the fell, and there's another shock in store for the Eden. Hellgill Force is the first major waterfall along the course of this mighty river. There's a public footpath where the occasional walker will let his booted feet splash by just feet away from the crag over which the river plunges. Down into a dark bowl, walls decorated with lush mosses, liverworts and ferns, verdant in this humid, sheltered place.

Already the waterway has gained in girth and can be called a river without any stretch of the imagination. Here, just below the tumbling mass of water at the Force, the Eden turns northwards for the first time. It picks up peat and silt from the surrounding land, gathering more water from other becks and gills as it rushes onwards, headlong between the great fells of Mallerstang. To the east of the Eden these fells roll along over the scarred length of Mallerstang Edge, while to the west the valley wall is formed by the broad swell of Swarth Fell and the sharp, stark outline of Wild Boar Fell.

Wildlife abounds here. Dippers find nesting caves behind stoppers in the water course, while grey wagtails flit along from boulder to boulder. In the summer months common sandpipers arrive from foreign climes and nest along its shingle banks.

On the river flows. Past Pendragon Castle beneath Little Fell. Nothing more than a small ruin today, Pendragon was built by Henry II and later came under the ownership of Lady Anne Clifford. Legend has it that Uther Pendragon, King Arthur's father, once held the castle. The setting is the most remarkable thing here today, especially the rough sweep of fellside that is Mallerstang Edge, dramatically carving the skyline along the east side of the dale.

By the time the Eden reaches Kirkby Stephen it is a proper, fully-fledged river. The town itself turns its back on the gushing course, as the river turns withershins around the houses and ducks beneath Frank's Bridge and then Lowmill Bridge.

Beyond Kirkby Stephen, and for the first time in its life, the River Eden has a confluence with another river, the River Belah. For the first time in its new life that is, for a river runs anew every day. New blood flows through its veins – water that is fresh from the fells, filtered daily through carboniferous caverns and by dense peat griffs. The Swindale Beck and Scandal Beck all merge into one within a distance of a mile or so of the confluence with the Belah, adding more weight and more clout to the eroding properties of the Eden.

The valley itself opens out here, though not exactly leaving the high fells behind, for further downstream the Eden will pass between the highest fells of the Pennines – Cross Fell, Great Dun Fell and Little Dun Fell, and the Northern Fells of the Lake District. It passes between these, rather than squeezes through, for the Eden Valley is now very wide indeed and holds some sizeable towns.

The river pushes through the fertile lands of the middle Eden Valley, mundifying the land, cleaning the banks and the flood plains as it scythes in half the town of Appleby-in-Westmorland. Houses of red Penrith fell sandstone turn their backs on the sometimes raging torrent, on the sometimes serenely garbling brook.

On again, in broad meanders, bypassing Penrith itself in favour of the lower lands that lie between the villages of Langwathby, Great Salkeld and Lazonby. The river here still has a fair amount of altitude – 250 feet or so above sea level, and not much horizontal distance in which to lose it before hitting the saltwater on the Solway Forth. It cuts a deep gorge through the soft, friable sandstone, the rock itself the bed of an ancient sea. The river gorge attracts oak and beech woodlands to clothe its flanks, and birds, badgers and deer find shelter within its confines. Red squirrels cling to the slopes of the gorge, and to their very existence, while kingfishers balance easily on wispy branches overhanging dark pools of the river.

The river here looks the colour of a good strong ale or porter. Perhaps Black Dub from the nearby Geltsdale Brewery. The peat has stained the waters themselves, giving more than a strong hint of mineral richness, while the dark colour itself is set off against the bright-red sandstone of the smooth-walled channels as it cuts into the riverbed. Flows. Forces. Stoppers. Kettle holes. Weird shapes etched into the delicate rock by the unyielding power of water. The power of the Eden.

The Eden dashes past the old mill at Armathwaite, then in its final stages mumbles along at a quite deceptive rate, by Wetheral and Warwick-on-Eden before plunging into the heart of Carlisle. Not far to go now, the river grinds over The Swifts as it gallops through Rickerby Park.

Just south of the Eden, in a subway that leads between Carlisle Castle and the city's Tullie House Museum, there stands a remarkable stone. It is a 14-tonne granite orb intricately engraved with a 16th-century diatribe against Border Reivers. The 1,069-word curse was originally aimed at the various Reiver families – the Armstrongs, Radcliffes, Salkelds, Hetheringtons and the Lowthers, among many others, who raided Carlisle and the Border areas of the north of England. Cattle rustling, blackmail, robbery, arson, kidnapping, murder and extortion were all an accepted part of their social system.

The Carlisle Cursing Stone was commissioned by city councillors for their millennium celebrations, and was created by Carlisle-born artist Gordon Young, at a cost of £10,000. However, since the work of art was installed, Carlisle and the north of Cumbria has suffered the worst local flooding for more than a century, the breaking down of local farming communities by the foot-and-mouth disease which hit the farms here particularly badly in the early part of this century, and a rash of local job losses as many factories closed down. Even Carlisle United, the city's football team, endured their own famine of goals, leading them to be relegated from the football league. Many people in Carlisle feel that this has all been brought about by the Cursing Stone. Local Councillor Tim Tootle even called for the stone to be destroyed, as he felt that the placing of a non-Christian artefact, based on an old curse on local families, was sure to bring bad luck to the city. Today, however, the Cursing Stone remains at the very heart of Carlisle.

Meanwhile, the River Eden takes its last few meanders just yards away, flowing gently and quietly to the sea. The tiny village of Rockcliffe overlooks the last bend in the river. Beyond this point, where the waters erode the banks of flaky red and orange sandstone, the River Eden becomes the Solway Firth, one of the greatest estuaries in Britain.

Where mudflats and saltmarshes are met, just below Rockcliffe village, there is a large nature reserve – Rockcliffe Marsh. On the north side of the marsh, another great river, the Esk, floods the flatlands of the Solway basin.

The Esk is in itself many rivers. Many courses drain through the Scottish Borders, carrying water from the fells. At the very head of Eskdale there lie the great rounded bumps of the Ettrick Fells. They crowd around the Ettrick Valley, which runs out into the Tweed and the North Sea, but at their backs these lovely hills fall in sweeping curves to form the headwaters of the White Esk.

Where the summit ridge of Ettrick Pen arcs north-eastwards in a graceful corrie-rim curve, a stream begins its life. Here all streams, seemingly all natural features, have wonderful-sounding names. This is the Muckle Cauldron Burn. It dashes down the steep hillside of Ettrick Pen in a white-water flash, plummeting playfully between the broken cliffs of Dobs Craig and Mitchell Hill, and then becomes the slightly more sedate Glendearg Burn.

Glendearg is the old Gaelic for 'red valley', though most of the names around these wild parts are Lowland Scots, not Gaelic at all. Names like The Shank, Foulbog, Bloodhope Head, Phawhope and Muckle Knowe. I love running my finger over the Ordnance Survey Landranger map, just searching out great, Border Scots names. Dumfedling always sounds to me like the feeling you have when you don't want to get out of bed in the morning, but can't quite explain why. It's a farm tucked in beneath the Forestry Commission plantations by the White Esk. Then there's Toddle Knowe, Macmaw Edge or Garwaldwaterfoot. Wonderful names to read. Wonderful names to say. Just sitting here at my desk writing these names makes me want to be in the Scottish Lowlands.

The hills of Eskdalemuir are dark, wooded places. Vast swathes of Sitka spruce, European larch, lodge pole pine, Douglas fir and Scots pine have been planted, row and column along their broad contours. Where open hillside exists the ground is rough. Grassy flanks dip and fold, covering bedrock of shales and mudstones. The Esk passes through the Scottish Borders and seems aloof.

It has another finger apart from the White Esk. Another vein, flowing in from the western reaches of the Castle O'er Forest, and known, perhaps not surprisingly, as the Black Esk, and where the two become one beneath the little bump of Downey Hill the main valley opens out into good pastureland. Langholm is the town of the Esk, the only town of any size, and the river forms a crucial heart to the lifeblood of the town.

Other rivers join the Esk – the Ewes Water at Langholm and the Liddel Water near Woodhouselees – then it's pell-mell for the bridge at Longtown, the last place of any consequence before Rockcliffe Marsh slows the river slightly, forcing it to take a final bend northwards as it enters the Solway.

5

Wintering on the Solway

The Solway's infant waters, the Rivers Eden and Esk, widen immediately at their confluence at Rockcliffe Marsh. A vastness of wild, flat merse, broad and long, cutting into the mudflats of the estuary, Rockcliffe Marsh is arguably the most important nature reserve on the Firth. The marsh is flat, at first glance at least, for here the close-cropped turf, sea-washed and saline, is bedded in silt brought down from the hills by the mighty rivers.

I walked along the banks of the Eden, my back to the village, while a band of comical oystercatchers skimmed into the gentle wind to my left and landed on a hump of mud, exposed by the low tide, on the opposite side of the channel.

Rockcliffe Marsh is primarily a bird reserve and is good both in summer and in winter. As it's by far the largest saltmarsh in Cumbria, the Cumbria Wildlife Trust has taken on the management of the reserve, although public access is restricted.

Summer on Rockcliffe Marsh is wonderful. As you approach the merse, skylarks and meadow pipits rise from their hidden cup-shaped nests, while lapwings, oystercatchers, redshanks and ringed plovers also nest on the saltmarsh. However, the most obvious breeding birds here are gulls and terns. There is a huge colony of breeding herring gulls and lesser black-backed gulls, while common and Arctic terns also find room to lay their eggs in relative privacy. It is because of these important numbers of breeding birds that access to Rockcliffe Marsh is by permit only during the summer months.

I walked along the public footpath that fringes the marsh on its southern side, and scanned across the flats with my telescope. I heard the larks singing brightly long before I managed to find one in my restricted field of view. He sang loudly and heartily as he climbed into the bright blue sky. Then, as skylarks do, he folded his wings and plunged back to earth again, gently parachuting the last few feet.

Over the levels of the merse, lapwings flew at gulls in agitation. Perhaps they felt threatened by the closeness of these big brutes, and no doubt there would be a fair amount of predation going on.

Winter is a very different kettle of fish at Rockcliffe, for then it is not that unusual for the entire Svalbard population of barnacle geese to descend on the merse – their numbers swelled by hundreds of pink-footed and greylag geese. Hen harriers quarter the flats looking for food, and occasional peregrines dash by, putting up large flocks of dunlin or redshank.

Another good winter wader site can be found at Browhouses, a little way westwards on the Scottish side of the Firth. The views stretch across the wide mouth of the River Esk where its peat-stained waters enter the Solway, to the distant purple smudge of the North Pennines.

Here on the mudflats there are usually large flocks of waders, including knot, dunlin, golden, grey and ringed plovers, lapwings and oystercatchers, while shelducks snuffle along the shelves of silt, pushing their bills through the mud as they sift for food.

However, I can't visit the north Solway without heading to either Caerlaverock or Mersehead. I've had so many great days at Caerlaverock, whether for ducks or geese in the winter or to see badgers or natterjack toads in the summer, that I've just completely lost track of the amount of times I've driven down the lane to Eastpark Farm. I always feel a sense of great excitement as I park the car, have a quick check of the bird feeders under a large birch tree to see if there are any unusual species having a feast there, and then head off onto the reserve.

On this northern side the Solway, knobbly hills clad on their lower slopes with forests, woods and plantation range down towards the coast in staggered ranks. South of the town of Dumfries, where the River Nith spills out into the Solway, the western wall of this river is formed by the rough, granite mound of Criffel. Rust-coloured vegetation spreads over this bald pate in the winter. If you look southwards from its summit plateau, you immediately notice how flat the coastal strip is. Merse and dune form the shoreline, and here you'll find Mersehead RSPB Reserve.

This is a superb place to spend a few hours, and as the reserve has a variety of interesting habitats, from lowland wet and dry grassland, to sand dunes, and from mudflats to mixed established woodlands, it is perhaps not surprising how there's always something worth seeing there. The RSPB bought Mersehead in 1993 as a working farm and have since worked hard to turn it into an important wildlife haven. The wet, grassy fields here are one of the most important places to see grazing barnacle geese but are also superb for farmland birds such as linnets, yellowhammers, skylarks and tree sparrows. There is a hide overlooking a large wader scrape from which you can often get good views of redshanks, lapwings and golden plovers probing for food, as well as a number of duck species.

Winter also brings peregrines flashing through the wader flocks, causing a mad scare and panic, putting the foolish hunted up in the air in wheeling flocks. This is, of course, the peregrine's intention, for the air is its hunting space. No peregrine would ever risk taking prey off the ground, as the speed of approach that is the peregrine's speciality would prove fatal if the bird misjudged the distance and hit the ground. In the air the peregrine is the master. Other birds of prey, such as merlins and hen harriers, hunt over the merse, and on a number of occasions I've come across a day-flying short-eared owl as I've sat patiently in the hide.

Just east of Mersehead, at the mouth of the River Nith, an array of mudflats with a rocky shore backed by sand dunes and maritime heathland give an inviting mix of habitats that bring more birds during the winter. Southerness Point is widely thought of as being one of the best wader hotspots on the estuary. Being a peninsula jutting across the mouth of the Inner Solway it can also be a great place for sea watching. I've often sat here and seen large numbers of divers, grebes and sea ducks, all gathering off shore in sizeable rafts.

I was at Southerness Point in January the year that we moved from the Highlands down to Cumbria. I was all wrapped up in dense layers of Paramo clothing, feeling snug and warm against the cold air. I scanned across from the lighthouse with my telescope and picked out large floating rafts of common scoters mixed in with a few rarer velvet scoters. Scaup were feeding closer in to the shore, while five red-throated divers worked the faster-flowing channels. Down on the shore a handful of ringed plovers picked daintily for food, while a flash of dunlin whirred by in synchronicity.

The south side of the Solway Firth is different in many ways. Obviously, the view is different, for the peaks of the Lake District fells that dominate the scene as you look south from the Dumfries side are not there when you gaze out from Cumbria. Criffel looks splendid when viewed from the south, and low, serene folds of green fields roll away to the distance.

Personally, I think the views of the birds are better from the Cumbrian side, too, but that is partly because there seem to be fewer people here, and certainly fewer towns and villages than on the Scottish bank. Another reason I always prefer birdwatching on the Cumbrian Solway is that the sun is always behind you as you stare out over the shining levels of mud and merse, sand and sea. The sun, when it shines, lights the birds' feathers, highlighting individual scallop-shapes on the brown back of a snipe or silver-edged plumage on a redshank's chest. You struggle to get these kinds of views from the north Solway coast, as the sun invariably blinds you.

The National Trust owns the large saltmarsh known as Burgh Marsh on the southern side. It is another of the main Solway sites for overwintering geese, ducks and waders, especially for large gaggles of barnacle geese as they forage along the merse. Curlews and golden plovers probe the muddy channels between the carpet of short grasses and thrift.

A minor road leads in a large loop from the red-sandstone village of Kirkandrews-upon-Eden around the area known as Beaumont, and I recently parked up here and walked out on a bracing day of bright skies and chasing clouds. The King Edward I monument, which stands in the middle of the marsh, gave me a focus for my short walk, and I stood for a while taking in the breathtaking big skies of the Solway.

To my right, towards the Pennines, Rockcliffe Marsh formed a foreground to the gentle swell of the fields and pastures that lie before the fells and moors themselves. A flight of lesser black-backed gulls bounced loose-winged on the stiff breeze, while a score or more dunlin flicked along just above the out-flowing tidal stream of the main channel of the Solway.

Westwards a minor road clings to the edge of the merse. It follows the course of Hadrian's Wall, although here there's not a great deal of this monstrous construction to see these days. A great little nature reserve lies right on the edge of the merse just west of Bowness-on-Solway village. Here old gravel pits have young oak and birch taking over the scoured sumps, and a number of little ponds have filled some of the pits. The reserve was given to the Cumbria Wildlife Trust in 1977 by Tilcon who had worked the gravel pits here for a number of years. Nowadays gorse and hawthorn scrub form dense areas on the reserve, in which passerines can shelter, while the ponds themselves give good feeding grounds for moorhens, mallards, pochards and snipe in winter.

A short walk leads around the reserve, and after my visit to Burgh Marsh I decided to head west to see what birds were around at Bowness. Even as I stepped from the car a jaunty pair of linnets jinked chirpily from the top of a nearby gorse thicket. Redpolls picked delicately between the tassels of birch trees, flicking out seeds with their tongues, while blue, great and coal tits seemed to be everywhere.

I walked clockwise around the path that encircles the main reserve, momentarily disturbing a roe deer doe who was munching the tough leaves of old dock stems. She glanced up and made to move away, and then remarkably decided that I was no threat to her at all and continued with her careful selection of leaves. I walked on spotting a couple of dozen twite on the fringes of the reserve, feeding on seeds strewn across the stubble of last season's cereal crop. This wonderland is as good a place as any hereabouts to spot tree sparrows, although on this particular walk I couldn't locate any in the dense undergrowth.

The ponds themselves were deserted – not even an odd mallard or moorhen pushing across the waters – so I headed back to the car and continued westwards to Campfield Marsh RSPB Reserve.

There are two distinctly different aspects to this reserve. To the north of the lane the saltmarsh and mudflats continue, and just west of the entrance to the reserve car park at North Plains Farm the RSPB have cleared open areas of

North Plains Farm, part of the Campfield Marsh RSPB Reserve

water on the merse itself to attract waders. Inland, to the south of the lane, vast acreages of arable farmland are backed by the South Solway Mosses National Nature Reserve.

Down on the saltmarsh there were lots of species of ducks, geese and waders, and I sat in the car with the window wound down to scan over the wader scrapes from the lay-by on the roadside. These scrapes are often good foraging grounds for pintail ducks, snipe and dunlin, and on that particular day these were all present. The pintail drakes looked great in the bright sunshine, their chocolate heads standing out against their pale bodies and white necks. Half a dozen snipe seemed to cuddle together on one edge of the scrape, although of course there was probably at least double that number on the merse that day.

That's the thing with snipe, they are designed to blend in, and they do it very well indeed. I remember on one occasion at a little reserve on the outskirts of Filey in Yorkshire. I'd been sitting in a hide with a small group of friends and together we'd clocked a couple of dozen species. Just as we were getting ready to leave the hide, someone spotted a brown blob camouflaged against a clump of aged sedges. We all crowded around the slits in the hide wall and realised that we'd been sitting within spitting distance of a snipe for half an hour or so, and had only just seen it. Then we noticed that there was another, and another. Three in total, and they'd blended in so well that we could so easily have missed them all.

The farmland at North Plains Farm is a Cumbria county stronghold of the tree sparrow – as I walked back from the little car park that nestles next to an old barn, I had a quick look on the bird table in the front garden of the farmhouse. There was a bit of a muddle of house and tree sparrows chirping from the hidden confines of a yellow-scale-covered elder, and a handful of chaffinches and greenfinches already on the table. Then a brazen blue tit swung by, grabbed a seed and vanished.

A public footpath leads through the farmyard, and here, by the barn at the end of the car park, I stopped briefly to have a look at the 'recent sitings' noticeboard. I followed the long, straight track, down through a row of hawthorn hedges to the first of the viewing screens that overlook the wet meadows on the farmland.

Fieldfares flew up in a multicoloured flourish from the top of an old ash tree, and a few bemused-looking redwings faltered for a few seconds, glaring down at me from behind their cream-coloured eye masks. Then they, too, were gone, flitting across the fields to a copse on the far side of the waterlands where holly, oak, birch and hawthorn awaited. Yet more birds of winter, visiting Britain's berry hedges when supply is short in their Scandinavian homelands.

The path leads to a large area of meadow which is used most winters by a large flock of pink-footed geese. The recent sitings board had me prepared for large number of geese here – 300 pink-feet and 560 barnacles it had reckoned. I sat in the new birdwatching hide that faces south over the wet grasslands and enjoyed the spectacle. I couldn't really say if the RSPB's figures were correct, but there were certainly plenty of geese about. A few wigeon 'wheeooo-ed' across the pastures, and teal joined in the cacophony from a nearby pool.

Way out to the left, as I gazed from the hide, I could see three roe deer grazing the lush grasses of the meadow where it fringed the heathery heathland of Bowness Common. In the distance, far beyond where the roe deer ate, a pale, ghostly shape stalled into the wind, dropping suddenly into the bed of ling and bell heather – a barn owl was out hunting early, making the most of the dry spell.

Further west still, the minor road leads onwards to Cardurnock village, a compact rash of old farmhouses and barns. The backs of these old farm dwellings overlooks the magnificent flats of Moricambe Bay. There's lots of mud and sand here – a build-up of silt carried along from the farmlands and dumped in the cove where the water backs up as it enters the Solway. The River Wampool flows serenely across the rippled sand and out into the Solway, and it is not unusual to see huge flocks of waders – especially golden plovers – working the mudflats for food. Shelducks sift busily through the sludge and sand, looking outsized, bulky and ungainly against the plovers, while curlews flute their 'curleewees' expansively across the bay.

North of Silloth, on the west Cumbria coast, a pebbly shoreline leads to a small peninsula jutting out into the Solway at the point where Moricambe Bay joins the main channel, known as Swatchway. This gorse-cloaked peninsula is Grune Point – a place well known among birdwatchers and twitchers as an important autumn migration hotspot.

The Solway Firth widens here – Grune Point forms the break between what is known as the Inner Solway and the Outer Solway. For me the Inner part of the Firth has always held the upper hand, both in terms of beauty and wildlife.

Across the Firth, the pudding-like form of Criffel dominates everything. A wonderful mountain in every respect. I stood at the old military lookout post on the Point, watching a peregrine struggling to force the wader flocks into flight on such a wild day. He drove in hard above their heads, swooping low at an incredible speed, and although there was an initial flurry, the waders – mainly redshanks, knot and a few grey plovers – soon settled down on the shore again. The great falcon was gone in a flash, leaving me wondering if perhaps he had nabbed a meal on his way through. The whole thing happened so quickly that I suppose he could have, although I certainly didn't see him carrying away his prey. Probably he was heading around to the Mawbray Banks further down the coast, hoping for a flight of dunlin or something.

In my eyes the Solway is possibly the most beautifully wild estuary in Britain. I love its closeness to the farmlands of North Cumbria, its proximity to the granite bulges of Criffel and, perhaps most of all, its big skies. Distant mountains of Lakeland and Dumfries add to the view, but by no means dominate it, and the sky – often set full of scudding grey clouds – amply fills the huge gap between their flanks.

6
Barnacle geese

Why am I so fascinated by barnacle geese? Well, the truth is, I'm not exclusively interested in them, any more than I am the other wildlife species that find a home, even temporarily, on our shores. Barnacle geese do have an amazing story to tell, though, and they are our link to the High Arctic, or at least one of many links that Britain, and Scotland in particular, have to the frozen wastes of the north.

Walking the saltflats of Mersehead or Caerlaverock at dusk, while a huge skein of prattling barnacles come in low over your head, fresh from Bear Island, is truly one of the many memorable spectacles of the natural world. Every time I walk the merse, I get a huge kick out of this miracle of nature. These birds return to the Solway every year, and bring with them a sense of the thrill of the wilder lands of the north.

The fact they these birds migrate northwards to the Arctic to breed on the short-cropped tundra has obviously not been fully understood throughout human history. In earlier times it was not known where the birds went during the summer months, and their sudden arrival in Britain each autumn was widely thought of as being one of the natural world's greatest mysteries. In fact, and incredibly, it was commonly thought that the barnacle goose came from a small marine crustacean, the goose barnacle. It was thought that as no egg or nest of the goose had ever been found, they must grow on the planking of ships and piers, emerging fully feathered from the shell of the goose barnacle, and it has to be said that there is a striking resemblance between the capitulum, the heart-shape of the shell of the barnacle, and the bill, head and neck of the goose.

Fortuitously, at a time when religious laws forbade the eating of meat on a Friday as well as throughout Lent, believing that the plump meat of the barnacle goose was from that of a sea creature, rather than being born of the flesh, was a great dietary advantage. For many people this was the only meat they would eat during fasts or on a Friday, and being readily available along suitable shores during the winter months, who could blame the folk of the estuaries for their beliefs? The tradition continued for many years, until Pope Innocence III forbade the eating of goose on Fridays. However, the practice continued for several centuries after his decree, particularly in the more remote parts of Ireland, where birds from the Greenland flock were considered a delicacy.

The barnacle goose is a true Arctic specialist, breeding nowhere else on the planet. There are three distinct populations of this species, and it is safe to say that members from each group very rarely mix with each other.

The barnacle geese that I'm most familiar with are those of the Solway Firth, between England and Scotland. The geese from this important population all breed in just one part of the world – Svalbard. So, they all spend their summers in that remote archipelago, and their winters on the calm shores of the Solway.

Another of the three groups breeds in east Greenland, and while these birds also migrate to Britain during the autumn, they do not make for the flat mud and sandbanks of the Solway. This group head for the west coast of Scotland, and in particular to the lovely whisky island of Islay, and also to the north and west coasts of Ireland.

The final group spend the summer on the islands of Novaya Zemlya, with a few scattered populations along the Russian Arctic coasts, and also some in the Baltic. These birds spread out over the White Sea, making for the coasts of the Netherlands and Denmark, and a few of these birds sometimes overshoot and find their way to the east coast of Britain.

In addition to these three populations, there are also about 1,000 or so naturalised birds that are resident in southern Britain, although it is believed that these are likely to be derived from captive stock, as escapees or released birds from wildfowl collections.

I love the fact that you can wander along the open shores of the Solway Firth or perhaps gaze out across the huge bay of Loch Indaal on Islay, and find barnacle geese by the thousand. And knowing that these same geese have their own patch that they will stick to fairly rigidly throughout the winter, then return to their own breeding grounds for the summer, is amazing.

There's something truly stirring about wild geese, their appearance either on the wing or on the gazing grounds is evocative of wildest places in the northern hemisphere. The strange yelping noises made by a skein of barnacles as they splash-land onto a nearby lake gets right under my skin, makes the hairs stand up on the back of my neck, and transports me immediately to the cold breeding cliffs of Svalbard.

Did I just say breeding 'cliffs'? Well, yes, that's another of the many strange things about barnacle geese that I find fascinating. They don't always make their nests on the ground as you'd expect, but instead can nest on ledges on inhospitable crags and scree slopes high above the starkly beautiful fjords of the Arctic. Those that do choose to ground-nest seem to prefer rock skerries and islets.

They lay four or five white eggs, although these soon yellow with dirt during the 24 days of incubation. The female has the job of sitting tight throughout this incubation period, while the male stays close by to guard the nest. Once the eggs have hatched, the chicks join their parents immediately in the search for food, and they leave the nest for good. The chicks stay with their parents as they forage for lush vegetation near freshwater pools, and after 40-odd days, the small bundles of downy feathers are ready to go it alone. Even then the fledglings don't turn their backs on their parents entirely. They'll remain as a family group until the following autumn migration, when they become separated on the journey south to the Solway. Three years later, when those same young barnacle geese are sexually mature, they will be pairing up ready to raise chicks of their own.

Numbers of barnacle geese on Svalbard have increased dramatically over recent years. It is known that there had been a huge decrease in the population there, until the 1940s when there were only a hundred or so pairs returning each summer from the Solway Firth. Overzealous hunting at both ends of their migration route had seriously depleted the Svalbard population, but now, thanks to international protection, and the work by the Wildfowl and Wetlands Trust, who have worked hard to secure winter feeding grounds around the Solway, the numbers are very healthy. In the winter of 2005 there were more than 27,000 individuals on the Solway, and the number is still increasing, albeit at a much slower rate.

I've watched geese coming into their winter roosts over a number of years, and not just barnacles on the Solway. Turning my mind back over the years I've been birdwatching, the first memory that springs to mind is the small group of brent geese that I spied as I drove slowly along the spit of sand to Spurn Point back in the early nineties. They were sifting through the mudbanks on the Humber side of the peninsula, and I had to reverse my car along the temporary track to get a second look. I'd probably assumed them to be Canada geese at first glance, for I was used to seeing them all over the place, but when I got the binoculars trained upon the seven or eight birds down by the shore I realised that they were something a bit special. These were wild geese, and a kind I'd not seen before. I remember having to have a look through my bird field guide, thumbing through the wildfowl section page by page to work out what species these were, and having a few moments of doubt while I spotted the subtle differences between the not hugely dissimilar barnacle geese and brent geese. And yes, these were definitely brents, and pale-bellied individuals, too, meaning that, according to my guidebook, they'd come down from either Svalbard, Greenland or Franz Josef Land for the winter. I now know that there is also another, dark-bellied race of brent geese. These birds breed in Siberia, or Alaska and Canada, and I was to come across a number of birds from this race on Islay during the preparations for this book.

I also recall the first time I came across barnacle geese. I was having a short walk in my local park in Hull, not far from where I then lived. Walking absent-mindedly through an avenue of trees, kicking autumnal leaves aside as I went, many still vividly coloured in bright shades of russet, vermilion, burgundy and gold, I just happened to glance over to my right and let my gaze fall on 16 dapper-looking birds grazing the short grass on a nearby football pitch. Again, the field guide came in handy when I got home, although I had a pretty good idea that these were barnacle geese even before I started thumbing through its slowly curling pages.

That's the thing with field guides. The more you thumb through them, turning from page to page as you try to remember the details of the bird you saw a couple of hours ago in the middle of the village duck pond, the better acquainted you become with all the other birds illustrated. You start off looking for, say, that duck on the village pond, having a vague notion that this particular one was quite small, certainly a lot smaller than the mallards that you know already, and seemed to have a yellow patch near its bum-end. You leaf through, closely examining the pictures of gadwall, wigeon, pochard, pintail, shoveler and the rest, eliminating them one by one when you realise that these birds are too large, and besides, don't have that distinctive yellow patch either. And then you find him, the drake teal. You read his description, and certainly some of it seems to fit. Perhaps you can't recall the bronzy-red-coloured head with its green flash. Then you read on and learn that the teal doesn't even quack like most other ducks. No this little chap whistles instead.

You immediately nip back out to the village duck pond to see if he is still there, taking your field guide and binoculars with you this time, and there he is. There are actually three of them. There's the yellow patch near the rear, and, yes, he does have a bronzy-red head with a green flash through it, although in the bad light it's quite hard to make this out. Your book tells you that the small, brown ducks that are hanging about with the drakes are in fact their mates, and within an hour or so, you've learned an awful lot about the teal, and had a jolly good morning's birdwatching too. You'll definitely recognise a teal again the next time you happen upon one, certainly the drake at any rate.

But, you've learned so much more from your morning's work. You've learned the subtle differences between the teal and gadwall. And also between the teal and the wigeon. And the pochard, pintail, shoveler, garganey, tufted duck and all the rest too.

The more you use your field guide to work out what that duck is, or that little brown and grey job at the bottom of the privet hedge, the more you'll become familiar with all the other birds in there too.

So, when I first came across those football-pitch-grazing barnacle geese in Hull's East Park, I had a pretty strong hunch that that was what they were even before I'd consulted my field guide, simply because I'd read their description while trying to sort out greylags from pink-footed geese, or perhaps those brents on the Humber from the common Canada geese that I'd seen practically everywhere since I was a child.

For a number of winters after that day I could pretty much guarantee that the same 16 barnacle geese would be around somewhere in the vicinity of East Park, and I'm pretty sure that these birds must come from naturalised stock. I suppose they could be Russian barnacles, overshooting their Netherlands' wintering grounds each year, but it seems a bit too much of a coincidence to be likely. Always 16 birds you see. The last time I saw them in East Park was during February 2005, and I dare say that they'll be there this winter, too, although possibly somewhat depleted in number.

Getting more and more familiar with the dark-season comings and goings of birds helps me to understand the importance of a good food source for these and all other birds.

Once the Arctic snows begin to build up in September each year, the ground-feeding birds – swans, geese, ducks and waders – simply can't find any food, and so they have to fly south to warmer climes. So, while our birds of summer are heading for the Med or Africa for their winter hols, other birds arrive on our balmy shores for the winter.

As I said earlier, it's not just barnacle geese that interest me. It's this coming and going of different bird species through the changing seasons. Worryingly, some birds are giving us a pretty clear indication that all is not well with the world. Some of our summer birds that would traditionally move south for the winter are now staying here throughout the year, finding that as the mean temperatures are actually getting warmer, they can find food aplenty. It is likely that many of our winter visitors will simply do the same in years to come and will not move to Britain for the winter.

That's one of the reasons that I wanted to travel to the Arctic, and to Svalbard in particular. The only way I could even hope to start getting to know more about our winter birds was to visit them on their own breeding grounds. It may not be so far down the line that many of these birds simply won't bother to make the journey south at all, but will instead choose to remain on the tundra as the wild wastes of the Arctic remain snow-free.

However, other animals that currently live the whole year round in the Arctic, such as polar bears, Arctic foxes, ivory gulls, walrus and scores more species, will probably die out – be lost for ever.

Even in Britain we stand to lose some of our own native species. We have some birds that are only just managing to cling on to their subarctic tundra habitat that remains only in a few tracts of wilderness in Scotland. Ptarmigan will probably retreat further and further north and will be lost in Britain to advancing global warming, as will the tiny snow bunting.

So that I could get my head around the possible loss of some of our own bird species, I wanted to go to the north to see them in their Arctic fastness. Svalbard was calling, and I wanted to follow the birds north as they left our shores in the spring.

A couple of months before I started on my journey north to Svalbard I called in at Caerlaverock for a chat with Dr Larry Griffin. Larry is the barnacle goose expert with the Wildfowl and Wetlands Trust and works out of a tiny office beneath the large tower hide on the reserve at Caerlaverock. I knocked on the door of his office and was admitted into the crazy mêlée of paperwork, maps, computer monitors, telescopes and reference books that was piled everywhere. I'd have been suspicious if the office had been clear and tidy. Larry was clearly a very busy, practical man.

He talked me through the migration routes that the barnacle geese took northwards in late April and May. Larry explained that a number of the geese at Caerlaverock had been fitted with satellite-tracking tags, and this had so far been a boon to his understanding of the behaviour of the birds, both while they were feeding around the various sites of the Solway and during their migration northwards.

On their journey to Svalbard in the early summer, for instance, Larry explained that, 'We just didn't know where the barnacle geese went between the time they crossed the Arctic Circle and when they arrived on their nesting islands further north.' Larry told me that since he started tagging the geese he's now discovered that the birds use a vital prebreeding feeding area beside a fjord in the south of Svalbard where the thaw starts earlier than elsewhere within the archipelago.

Another fascinating fact that the tagging survey has thrown up is the speed with which these birds can fly when migrating. In 2007, the Wildfowl and Wetlands Trust discovered that the geese could cross the North Sea – a distance of 300 miles – in just 5 hours! One particular tagged bird, named Barbow, crossed over to Norway with an average speed of 80 miles per hour with the aid of a strong back wind, although as Larry pointed out that as the satellite tag is only capable of recording at 80 as a top speed, Barbow could actually have travelled even faster at times. Barbow was one of two barnacle geese caught and tagged at Newfield Farm on 23 March 2007, and soon after he was heading north making his record-breaking flight to Svalbard.

He eventually made for the breeding grounds above a Polish research station that sits on the north shore of a spectacular fjord on the island of Spitsbergen, the main island of Svalbard. This fjord, the Hornsund, is ringed by snow-capped peaks and huge fangs of rock, and my journey to Svalbard would take me to Barbow's breeding grounds later in the same season.

After breeding Barbow moved slowly southwards through the coastal fringes of Spitsbergen over a period of two months. Then on 4 September, at 10 a.m., he began heading south for warmer climes. He arrived at Bjørnøya, often known as Bear Island, at 2 p.m. that same afternoon. Barbow then spent nearly three weeks feeding on the snow-free tundra on the high plateau at the south-eastern corner of the island, making just one flight over to the west coast on 12 September and returning to the east the following morning.

At 9.32 p.m. on 24 September, Barbow was last recorded on Bjørnøya – he had resumed his journey southwards once more. Four days later, he arrived on the Norwegian coast just south-west of Tromsø, and was last recorded in the same region on 6 October. It's now two months later, as I am writing this, and Barbow has not been recorded again since. We shall probably never know what became of him, although we owe him a great debt. Without these satellite-tagged birds, we could never hope to understand where birds go during migration.

Other barnacle geese make the journey south to the Solway in one continuous flight. One particular bird, known as Braveheart, left Svalbard on 26 September at about 10 a.m. He completely bypassed Bjørnøya, where it had previously been thought the majority of geese stopped off to feed on their southward journey. By 7 a.m. on the 28th he'd arrived in Scotland, having flown over North Berwick, and was resting at Aberlady Bay that morning. The weather conditions were good, though, and he seemed keen to resume his journey to the Solway Firth, and within four hours he was resting on Blackshaw Bank just off the shore at Caerlaverock. By that afternoon Braveheart was feeding on the saltmarsh of the reserve with another 2,650 birds that had arrived over the previous 24 hours.

7

Setting sail for the north

Rain pelted hard against the windows of the train. It pulled to a sudden stop at the end of the line in Oban, and while people crowded to the doors, grabbing rucksacks, suitcases, laptop bags, babies in pushchairs and toddlers in tantrums, I just sat there wondering if the rain might ease at all. The absurdity of this situation came home to me as I watched the other passengers, now out on the platform, struggling to pull jacket hoods up in the wind, while umbrellas where whipped inside out in comic fashion. The rain was as persistent as it had been for weeks, although it had at least eased into more of a drizzle.

These people just put up their hoods against it all and got on with their lives. My sitting there waiting for it all to stop seemed pathetic by comparison. This was Scotland after all, and weather like this is not uncommon. And besides, I had come up to Oban to board a ship for the Arctic. It was June, and I was going in search of the barnacle geese of the Solway. I wanted to catch up with them on their summer breeding grounds, and although I realised that I would probably not find Barbow or any of the other birds tagged by the Wildfowl and Wetlands Trust, I secretly hoped that I might. I laughed to myself, thinking that if I couldn't hack this bit of Scottish smirr, then what the hell was I doing heading to Svalbard!

The MV *Grigoriy Mikheev* is a multinational ship. She was built in Finland and first saw service as a Russian spy ship during the cold war. A Dutch company, Oceanwide Expeditions, now owns her, although it was through the London offices of an Australian company, World Expeditions, that I had booked my trip.

The captain of the ship, Aleksandr Pruss, was Russian, whereas most of the crew were either Russian, Polish or Turkish. The chefs were both Danish, while the doctor was German, and the purser, Angel Quiroga Iturralde, was Basque. There were two wildlife guides on board, Martin Grey from the Orkney Islands, and Mick Brown from Ireland, though Mick now lives in Wales. As I say, a truly multinational crew.

We left Oban in dense, low cloud. A definite dreich. A few fishing boats coasted in and out of the harbour, while the Mull ferry slipped out just ahead of us. The sky was grey and very dull, but at least the rain had now stopped. I stood on the top deck as we passed calmly around the northern tip of Kerrera. Behind us, the mad folly of MacCaig's Tower flaunted itself above the town, while a stream of common terns passed through the Sound of Kerrera. The Firth of Lorn was as tranquil as I'd ever seen it, skulking as it was below the mass of grey that was the sky. A few other passengers had joined me on deck to watch the passing of the Scottish mainland. There was the usual staid sizing up of each other among the passengers, and we timidly pointed out flotillas of guillemots and razorbills to each other as we slipped gently by.

There were quite a few gannets in the Sound of Mull, which was interesting to see as the nearest breeding colony is way out to the west of the Outer Hebrides on St Kilda, and being late June I'd have thought they'd all have been on nests. Mind you, gannets do travel great distances to feed, so perhaps the calmer waters of the Inner Hebrides had drawn them in. For a bird that hunts by following shoals of fish, hurling itself into the broiling sea in an often successful attempt to bag one, I guess being able to see the fish in the first place is a great bonus. So calmer waters suited these gannets. Arctic and common terns followed the ship, and a few Manx shearwaters scooted stiff-winged across the steely-grey flats of the Sound.

As the dull light began to fade over the Small Isles later that evening, I ventured on deck once more to catch the last of the day before it became engulfed by nightfall. The stark headland of Ardnamurchan cast a dark smudge against the vague horizon where two tones of grey met, and the lighthouse beam pierced the dusk then faded. Again, pierced the dusk then faded. Then all seemed dark. Scotland was gone. Greyness surrounded us, and we ploughed on into its depths.

Tomorrow would bring new islands. Outposts of the British Isles. Islands of the North Atlantic.

Eight weeks or so before I'd slipped out of Oban on the *Grigoriy Mikheev*, there'd been a strange calling from the north. The daylight hours had lengthened. Warmer air currents had carried on the wind to the wide seascapes of the Solway Firth.

The birds there had become restless. They'd flocked together in big groups, flying around the estuary in ragged skeins, flitting from one grazing site to another. Something was stirring within them, and they'd very soon feel the need to venture northwards, the climbing sun to their backs, to where they'd get together with their mates, ready to raise a fresh brood of chicks.

One of the biggest congregations of barnacle geese was on Rockcliffe Marsh. Barnacle geese had come in to the merse in immense squadrons, sometimes hundreds or thousands strong. They were joined by other birds, such as whooper swans, also preparing for a similar journey to the north. Around 25,000 of these magnificent birds make the flight down to Britain from their breeding grounds in Iceland, with about 500 or so spending the winter at various sites around the Solway.

Waders were gathering, too, with large numbers of curlews and redshanks, golden plovers and lapwings feeding alongside the 'nashgabbing' geese. There had been a feeling of great excitement among the flocks. A feeling that a momentous journey was in the planning.

I was ready to follow the birds northwards. It would not be possible for me to follow the exact route taken by the barnacle geese as they retraced their flyway to Svalbard, but I knew I'd be able to explore some of their stopping off points during my own journey.

Left: Barnacle geese

Below right: Barnacle geese
in formation arrive on the
Solway

Bottom: Barnacle geese
arriving on the Solway

A newly hatched
lesser black-backed
gull on North Rona

Barnacle geese at
Mersehead RSPB
Reserve

Barnacle goose on a
frosty morning

Left: Shelduck on ice

Below: Shelduck, mallard and gulls

Teal standing on ice

Whooper swan

Wigeon walking on ice

A grey seal on the Scottish island of North Rona

Above: Exploring North Rona

Left: Puffin on North Rona

Gannet colony on Sula Sgeir

Gannets on their breeding cliffs, Sula Sgeir

Great Skua on Unst, Shetland

Great Skua on Yell, Shetland

Otter on Shetland

Knot on the beach on Jan Mayen

Torshavn, capital of the Faroes

MV *Grigoriy Mikheev* anchored off the Faroes

Top left: The stunning scenery of Jan Mayen

Top right: Mountains of Burgabukta in the Hornsund

Left: The wilderness of the Hornsund, on the island of Spitsbergen

Laval hills on Jan Mayen

Loch Gruinart on the island of Islay

The MV *Grigoriy Mikheev* at anchor below the Hornsundtind

Male polar bear crossing pack ice in Storfjorden

Perfect weather in the Hornsund

An ivory gull on Spitsbergen

A glaucous gull, one of the largest gulls of the Arctic

Little auk on Spitsbergen

Little auk on its nesting site
above the Polish Station in
the Hornsund

A black guillemot is
inquisitive about our
boat on the Hornsund

Loch Indaal from Bowmore on Islay

Purple sandpiper

Barnacle geese at Loch Gruinart on Islay

8

North Atlantic islands

A following sea and an easy swell carried us northwards through the night along the western seaboard of Scotland. Up on the monkey deck before breakfast I'd spotted two lumps in the North Atlantic, quite a way ahead of us. These two islands, North Rona and Sula Sgeir, I had wanted to visit for such a long time, having looked across the miles of ocean that separate them from Shetland, Orkney and mainland Scotland.

The first stop for us was to be the vast gannetry of Sula Sgeir. Martin briefed us after breakfast, explaining that the captain would endeavour to get the ship as close to Sula Sgeir as possible. We wouldn't be landing, as this is very difficult, and in any case the island is a nature reserve, but he did think it likely that we'd get close enough for good views of the 6,000 or so gannets that gather there to breed. Martin also explained that he'd recently spotted an unlikely visitor in among the gannets.

Back up on deck we all gathered in the bright morning sun eager to make the most of our first island of the trip. Even from a few miles distance gannets wheeled in the air above the ship, while scores more came by in long white lines from their fishing grounds. Perhaps some of these were the same birds we'd seen the evening before in the Sound of Mull.

The island is a narrow, goose-neck shape, and its name means, appropriately enough, gannet skerry. Great cliffs fall from the gannet-heavy top, and there is only one place where it is safe to land on the island, and even then only in calm seas. That doesn't deter the men of Lewis, though, from undertaking every year one of the most hazardous journeys to be taken in British waters. Each September, open boats are launched from Ness, the northern point of the Outer Hebrides, and the men cross the 51 miles of the North Atlantic in search of guga or young gannets. Although this is a nature reserve, a special licence is granted so that the Lewismen can keep their traditional hunt for what used to be an important food source.

The flesh of the guga is oily and tastes, not surprisingly, of fish, or at least so I am told. I've only once seen guga meat, and that was in a private store in Stornoway. It was pickled and looked like a stinking brown mass of obscure body parts, crammed to the brim of a jar. On Lewis it is considered to be a great delicacy, but I'm positive that it must be an acquired taste. Peering into that murky specimen jar in Stornoway, I was convinced that it was a taste I wouldn't want to acquire.

The men of Lewis arrive at Sula Sgeir as the fledgling gannets are just about ready to leave the nest. Many may have gone already, and at that stage the young birds are old enough to swim and fish, but not old enough to fly. They simply bob around on the sea, and to harvest them all the Lewismen need do is pluck them from the surface.

Those that aren't gathered from the sea are taken from the nests themselves. The boats are tied up to a metal ring, drilled into the base of the cliffs at Geodha a' Phuill Bhàin, the only safe landing spot on this perilous rock. No other anchorage is available, the rest of the skerry being ringed by cliffs. Once on the rock the men live for a few days in a group of tiny stone bothies while they are busy harvesting. Once their annual quota is reached, they haul their catch into the boats and begin the long journey home, southwards across the North Atlantic to Ness on Lewis.

When I first heard of the annual guga harvest on Sula Sgeir I was shocked to say the least. Two thousand young gannets harvested from an adult population of about six thousand seems an awful lot. That said, the population here seems stable, and of course the Lewismen are careful not to overharvest as that would have a detrimental effect on years to come.

From the monkey deck of the *Grigoriy Mikheev* we could see the stone bothies that the guga-hunters use, high up above the cliffs in a notch on the skyline. We could also make out the landing place at Geodha a' Phuill Bhàin, and I tried to imagine coming to this far corner of the seas in a little rowing boat, approaching the great stacks with care, then leaping from the boat onto slippery rocks beneath the enormous cliffs. A rough scramble would lead to the top of the cliffs, and up there you'd find no vegetation or water to sustain you during your few days on Sula Sgeir.

Gannets wheeled around the cliffs, coming in to land from the south and floating on the updraught high above the calm seas. A few grey seals bobbed around the base of the cliffs, and we each scanned among the gannetry with binoculars, searching for the rare bird that Martin had told us we might be lucky enough to spot here.

For a number of years there had been a black-browed albatross hanging out with the gannets that returned each summer to Scotland. Between 1967 and 1969 one had been present on Bass Rock in the Forth of Firth, then from 1972 until the mid 1990s there was another, possibly the same bird, over at Hermaness National Nature Reserve on the island of Unst, way up on the northern tip of the Shetland Isles. Even prior to this individual turning up on Bass Rock in 1967, there had been another albatross, and many people feel that it is likely to have been Albert, in Iceland during July 1966.

These huge birds are usually found in the deep south of the Southern Ocean and don't usually venture north of the equator. However, Albert, as he inevitably became known, was thought to have strayed too far north and got mixed up with a band of gannets who were heading up to Scotland to breed. He joined the throng and stayed with them for many years, even trying his best to mate with any female gannet that happened to take his fancy.

Back when Olivia and I had first met up in these Northern Isles, we'd walked out to the cliffs at Hermaness, being dive-bombed by bonxies as we crossed the moor. Puffins peered out of their burrows at us just inches from where we sat, and we'd walked along the cliffs to the crag known as Saito, for this was where Albert was then reputed to have been hanging out. We scanned every ledge but couldn't see him.

In the 1990s, Albert the Albatross vanished from Hermaness, and many birdwatchers believed that he must have died. Then, a couple of years ago, a natural history group, on a ship just like the *Grigoriy Mikheev*, happened to be scanning the gannet colony on Sula Sgeir when they spotted something very unusual. A black-browed albatross was occupying a ledge right in among the nesting gannets.

And there he was. Exactly where Martin had said he would be. Looking slightly bemused (frustrated even!), seemingly eyeing up his female neighbours.

For a while back in the late 1970s, ornithologists speculated that Albert might actually have been a female bird. From 1976 onwards the bird built a nest at Saito, but it never laid eggs. It is now known that both sexes of black-browed albatrosses take part in the nest-building process, and it is agreed that if Albert was female, infertile eggs would most certainly have been laid during this period.

Of course, we will never know if this bird now in the North Rona–Sula Sgeir group of islands (for Martin has seen the albatross on both islands, and told us that he saw it flying between the two on one occasion during 2006) is the same albatross that first turned up in Iceland all those years ago, or indeed if that was also the same bird that lived at Hermaness for such a long time, but we do know that this species is especially long-lived. Albert was last seen at Hermaness on 7 July 1995, which, assuming that he was that same individual from Iceland, would have made him at least 32 years old back then. If this huge-winged bird on Sula Sgeir was our old friend, he would now be at least 41 years old, and still going strong. We also know just how lost a black-browed albatross would have to be to make it this far north, so it seems possible that this is indeed Albert, and that he's been with us for some time now. And at last, after many walks out over the moor at Hermaness to poke my head over the cliff tops at Saito, all of them in vain, I had finally caught up with him.

Captain Aleksandr nosed the *Grigoriy Mikheev* gently around the cliffs of Sula Sgeir, giving us all plenty of time to appreciate the impressive spectacle of thousands of gannets circling above us, sitting on nests, plunge-diving into the cold waters of the North Atlantic, and bringing back catches from fishing grounds further afield.

The weather was getting better by the minute, and we could clearly see our next destination 11 miles away to the north-east.

North Rona is a very special island and has a very special feel to it when you walk its grass-topped crown.

We went ashore in Zodiac boats, eight passengers per craft. Martin and Mick had been out first to make a reconnaissance of the possible landing sites and had decided on a little rocky cove on the east side of the island.

A narrow neck of land connects the main part of the island to a long, low finger to the north known as Fianuis, and we came ashore at Geodh' a' Stoth, the bay on the east side of this narrow neck.

Thrift bloomed bright and pink on the short sward and birds were everywhere. We walked westwards to the far side of the neck, picking out a few pairs of puffins nesting in wide cracks in the rocks of the low cliffs on the far side.

Grey seals breed here in large numbers, with more than 7,500 coming ashore each autumn to give birth. Most years see around 2,500 pups born on North Rona alone, making it one of the most important breeding colonies in Britain. There were a handful on shore as we crossed the island, climbing beyond the puffin's cliffs to Mullach a' Bhaile, the broad, grassy hill on the western side of Rona.

Landing by Zodiac on North Rona

Wheatears danced from rock to rock, showing us the white arses that gave them their old name. It was, of course, the Victorians who changed this to wheatear – they could never use a name so vulgar!

Swallows and swifts contoured the air stream that hung around Mullach a' Bhaile's flanks, and at the top we caught sight of another unusual migrant bird. A cock Lapland bunting, perky as anything, bright in his prebreeding plumage and definitely on the pull, had found this remote outpost and was feeding up prior to continuing on his journey. He, too, was heading north to his breeding grounds, and possibly, like us, also heading for Svalbard. Lapland longspurs, to give them their much chirpier name, also nest in Greenland, northern Canada and Alaska, nearly always in the higher latitudes including Arctic Norway and the remote islands of Franz Josef Land, and also the Russian Arctic islands of Novaya Zemlya and Severnaya Zemlya. They have even been known to nest in Scotland.

Over the crown of Mullach a' Bhaile and the tallest lazy-beds I've ever seen, now grassed over and sad-looking, led down to the old village site.

The first inhabitant of North Rona is said to have been St Ronan, who built a hermitage on the island in the 8th century, but it does seem likely that there were people here before the saint ever arrived.

From 1680, there is a record of a visit to North Rona by the Reverend Donald Morison. He found five families living a harsh existence on the island. Stone houses, thatched to keep out the rain and cold, provided shelter for each family, and there were storehouses, cattle-sheds and barns too. The people seemed content to the Reverend, and he commented that they took their names from the colours of the sky, rainbows and clouds. They did have some contact with the outside world, albeit only the northern tip of Lewis, the Ness area, which they visited very occasionally. As a community they had decided to restrict their population to 'thirty souls', by sending their 'supernumerary' people on to Lewis.

The 1680 report states that soon after the Reverend came, there was a plague of rats from a visiting ship. The rats ate what little food was stored on the island, and shortly after this some passing seamen killed the island's only bull. Within the space of a year, the inhabitants of North Rona had been wiped out.

The sad end to this race of island-dwellers was only discovered when a group from St Kilda were shipwrecked on North Rona after a big storm had carried them from their own waters. The St Kildans lived on the island for seven months, spending the time building a boat out of driftwood. This they then sailed to Stornoway.

The island was resettled from Lewis, but by 1796 only one family remained, the rest apparently had drowned in a fishing accident. The family were shepherds, the MacCagies, and when a Dr MacCulloch landed on North Rona in 1815, the whole lot of them, Kenneth, the shepherd, his wife, three children, and his deaf mother, fled and hid. They said that they'd 'seen no face' for seven years, and feared that MacCulloch was either a pirate or an American!

Kenneth MacCagie managed the sheep flock on North Rona for an annual wage of £2 worth of clothing. There was no boat kept on the island, so that he couldn't leave without permission from the owner, MacLeod of MacLeod. The family home was mainly underground, and they lived on a diet of fish and potatoes. They left in 1820.

The next shepherding family came to North Rona in 1829. John MacDonald brought his wife Cirstina and his daughter Catherine, and the couple had three more children, all of them born on the island. The family left for Lewis in 1834.

By 1844, North Rona had a single inhabitant, Donald MacLeod, the self-styled 'King of Rona'. He was eventually evacuated, and, in 1850, the island was offered for use as a penal settlement to the government, free of charge. This offer was rejected.

Finally, during the years 1884 to 1885 the last inhabitants of the island arrived. Two men from Ness travelled to North Rona to start a new life there. They'd had an argument with the minister on Lewis, and they'd vowed never to return to the parish. Were these men homosexual? Were they forced to leave Lewis and banished to this remote island as a penance? Of course, we'll never know, but the rumours on Lewis to this day seem to suggest as much.

In February 1885, a boat was sent out to check on the health of these two men. They were both found dead, one from natural causes, the other, it is said, from 'exhaustion after nursing his friend'.

We ambled around the old village site, enjoying the noise of hundreds of starlings busily nesting in the ruined dykes and the remains of the stone buildings. Petrels also nest in among the old walls, both the tiny, martin-sized storm petrel, and the slightly larger Leach's. These remarkable little seabirds feed far out at sea and only return to the nest site during the cover of darkness.

The village site traces its origins back to the Norse settlers of the 8th century, but the centrepiece, and for many people the main reason for coming to North Rona (not that many people do come here), is the Chapel of St Ronan.

The Royal Commission on the Ancient and Historical Monuments of Scotland lists the chapel as one of the three oldest structures of the Celtic Church, and it is believed that this little ruined chapel is probably the oldest relatively unaltered building in British Christendom. Relatively unaltered in that it is known that when Frank Fraser Darling stayed here in the 1930s he claimed to have rebuilt part of the chapel.

So who was St Ronan? Well, that's actually a bit of a sticky point. Donegal had no fewer than twelve saints known by that name, and Scotland had at least two. There are dedications to St Ronan on both Islay and North Uist, and whether this island took the name of the saint, or vice versa, is another contentious issue.

The remains of St Ronan's Chapel on the island of North Rona

What is known is that there was a 6th century cross on the site next to the chapel. This was removed in the 1930s and taken to the Teampull Mholuaidh at Erropaidh on Lewis, but it is thought that it marked this particular St Ronan's grave.

I walked through the village, marvelling at the sad remains, and wondering what life must have been like on this once very fertile island. Beneath derelict boundaries, fulmars now nest in the shelter provided by walls once raised by hard toil, while great black-backed gulls have commandeered the better nest sites around the lazy-beds. I ducked low to crawl into the compact chamber of the chapel. Martin was in there quietly gathering his thoughts.

'I came in here last year and had a remarkable experience,' he told me. Martin's a big, burly, no-nonsense kind of a chap. Brought up on North Ronaldsay in the Orkney Isles, he looks like he's spent a lifetime working the sea and the land. Rough, but with an easy smile, I can't imagine him speaking lightly about any spiritual happenings.

'Aye,' he went on. 'Came in here with a small group one day. They had a look around, took a few photos and then left me to it.'

My eyes were becoming accustomed to the dark interior by now, as only thin shafts of light penetrated the broken stonework walls. I could see him smiling, to himself, not to me. He seemed almost to be talking to himself.

'I'd closed my eyes for a few minutes, to just breathe quietly and to be still.

When I opened them there was a bright cross shining on the wall at the end there.' He waved his arm vaguely towards the back of the cell.

'Nearly shit myself,' he laughed. 'Then I realised that it was just the sun shining through the stones.'

We laughed together, but I could tell that for him this place does have some kind of spiritual significance. Some kind of draw that brings him in here time after time, to just stand and be quiet.

I left the group milling around the long-dead village – dead of human life that is, but now reclaimed by the starlings and fulmars. People quietly photographed the replica cross that now stands where the old one of St Ronan once marked his grave, and the chapel that crumbled alongside. Martin snoozed contentedly atop one of the lazy-beds, and Mick scanned the sea for birds with his binoculars.

I followed one of the lazy-beds uphill, towards the western flank of Mullach a' Bhaile. Great black-backed gulls were everywhere, and for each menacing pair circling close above my head I carefully scanned the ground for signs of their nests. Some had eggs still in them, lying snugly against the nest walls lined with grass, while others had chicks in them, scrawny and ugly.

Bonxies were all over the moors too. These large, bullish brutes are possibly one of my favourite seabirds. They are mean, ugly, have atrocious eating habits, and nearly everyone else hates them, but for me this is one of the birds that makes me feel truly alive whenever I get near them. Their other, so-called common name, is the great skua, although I've never actually heard anyone call them that. The thing is you only really get them up here in the north, and certainly, in Scotland at any rate, they go by their local dialect name, bonxie. It's much more appropriate than 'great skua' which doesn't tell you anything at all about the bird. Bonxie does the job perfectly, describing what happens to you if you get too close to them on their nesting grounds. They swoop in and bonk you on the head. Or at least they pretend to. That's what I like to think gives them this name, although in truth I know that it comes from the Old Norse 'bunksie', which, rather prosaically, just means 'dumpy body'.

I've been clouted by them on a number of occasions, and I think it's great fun, so long as you're not keeping them off the nest for too long or stopping them feeding their young. To walk carefully over a breeding moor, making sure not to tread on any eggs or chicks, is one of life's finest pleasures. Most other people I've taken onto bonxie moors are generally terrified, but you do get the odd one or two that love it, and then together we share a rare thing. A love of the bonxie, and its piratical ways.

The other thing that people find disgusting about bonxies is the way that they hunt. Or rather, the way that they don't hunt. No, what bonxies do is keep a careful eye on the hunting habits of other birds, gulls for instance, and as soon as they see another bird with food they begin the chase. They'll harass a gull, even great-blackies or herring gulls, brutes themselves, the bonxies aggressively feigning attacks, relentlessly dive-bombing and even pecking at wing-tips and feathers until the poor gull just gives up and either drops its snack or vomits it. Then the bonxie can have its meal.

Another successful bonxie method of getting food, and this one is a hunting strategy, is to sit on a cliff top or a ledge and to dive-bomb puffins as they come in off the sea. I've known a bonxie swallow a puffin whole. Now that's a big meal, even for a bonxie. And yet I still love them. I guess someone's got to. The way I feel about bonxies is that they must be filling an ecological niche somehow, as with all other birds, mammals, insects or whatever. They must be part of the big scheme of things. Just because they are not cute, like a puffin say, it doesn't mean that they don't have as much right to eke out a living as those sandeel-murdering auks! OK, so I'm stretching the point, but you can see what I mean.

As for stealing food off gulls, well, since when did herring gulls become lovable? The point is I love to see all animals, even those red in tooth and claw, doing what they are designed to do best. And bonxies are designed to bully and terrify other birds. Oh yes, and people too.

I stopped and chatted for a while with Mick, our Irish guide. We marvelled together at a pair of whooper swans that circled the island over and over again, the whole time we were there. A couple of golden plovers piped from the top of the hill, while a thin-nosed wedge of whimbrel, five birds in all, flew north over our heads.

From the top of Mullach a' Bhaile I looked down onto An Sithean, a broad, grassy col. This was heavily guarded by bonxies and a few Arctic skuas. Just downhill from the top of the hill was a green shed, looking very odd and out of place on this tiny island in the middle of nowhere. It was an open bothy, used by researchers who come here from time to time to monitor the marine life or the bird life on the island. It looked reasonably comfortable inside and would make a good base for anyone planning to spend some time here. I guess you'd probably have to get permission from Scottish Natural Heritage, who manages North Rona and Sula Sgeir together as a National Nature Reserve. North Rona is actually owned by the Barvas Estates on Lewis, and I suspect that you probably need permission from them also if you want to land here.

On the other side of the col, the land rises in easy contours to the highest point of the island. I walked across the col, enjoying the bonxies and Arctic skuas nesting there. Six golden plovers winged away towards Fianuis, and a wheatear bobbed along the cliff-tops as I climbed to the summit of Toa Rona, at 108 metres above sea level, the highest part of North Rona.

On the cliffs themselves a few puffins clowned around on thrift-covered ledges, while meadow pipits seemed to be everywhere. Swifts floated savagely by on the thermals, slicing the air currents with their scythe wings. A few swallows were there, too, and I even spotted a house martin. It seemed as though migration fever was certainly in the air.

I started counting the meadow pipits, surprised at how many appeared to be along the cliff-top. I reached 40, and then gave up. Obviously there had been a fall of migrating birds and there could well have been thousands of these little grassland passerines on the island.

Another avian surprise was a pair of siskins that hopped around a little rocky bluff. Bearing in mind that these tiny finches are usually to be found in the tops of conifer trees or perhaps picking seeds from birch tassels, this was the last place I had expected to see them, on a tree-less island in the North Atlantic.

I glimpsed cautiously over the cliffs just below the lighthouse that adorns the top of Toa Rona. There is a big gulf in the cliff-line, known as Geodha Mairi, and the *Grigoriy Mikheev* gave the huge numbers of guillemots, razorbills and puffins that came off the cliffs in great wheeling masses something to use as a roundabout. There didn't seem to be much giving way to either right or left, though, as the frantically fishing auks prepared for the raising of their young.

Back at Geodh' a' Stoth the group were gathering ready to be taken back to the ship. I came down the slopes from the eastern flank of Mullach a' Bhaile slowly, accompanied by Martin who was also watching the swifts contouring the hillside in impressive glides.

A drift of Arctic and common terns took off from the peninsula of Fianuis as we met the group, donning life jackets and wellies in readiness for the Zodiac passage back to the ship. A grey seal flopped languidly just a few feet away, and I for one was very sad to be leaving this magical place. North Rona had cast her spell on me, and I wanted to spend time with her, alone in the wild North Atlantic.

9
Simmer dim

We motored through the choppy waters in the channel of Nólsoyarfjødur, the seaway that lies between the green islands of Nólsoy and Streymoy. Streymoy is the main island of the Faroes group, and now we were heading out of the capital city of Torshavn, having spent the morning exploring its streets.

First view of the Faroes, through the cabin window

The harbour and old quarter of Torshavn are fascinating. Mick led us on a walk around the fortified headland that guards the entrance to the harbour, while black guillemots and eider ducks fished, and Arctic terns plunged daintily into the shallow water on the shoreline. Venturing further into the city, we found a lovely harbour, though on such a sunny day we felt like we were definitely seeing it at its best. I tried to imagine the same scene after a whale hunt, when the clear waters run red with the blood of scores of pilot whales, herded into these same peaceful bays to be slaughtered.

A few of us wandered on, through streets of timber-framed houses with birch-bark roofs, then up to the town's Natural History Museum, which seemed to be mainly concerned with how to kill things and eat them. For me the main interest in the museum was the sad remains of a great auk.

This huge member of the auk family, the same family that includes puffins, guillemots and razorbills, was hunted to extinction. The last known great auk was killed in 1844 on the island of Eldey, just off the south-east coast of Iceland.

These giant razorbills once covered quite a large area, with a line between Spitsbergen and Greenland being the northern limit of their range. Their main problem was that they had developed a design fault. They had evolved, like penguins, to be flightless. Obviously, they had evolved in this way so that their wings could be used as very effective paddles for swimming, and they were well adapted to catching fish.

Unfortunately, being flightless had made them very easy to catch on land, and they formed a valued addition to the diet of explorers and fishermen. As often happens with food sources that are readily available, easy to collect and tasty, too, the great auk stocks were massively exploited. Ironically, as the great auks became scarcer, they increased in market value as collectors and academics, who felt that they simply had to have one in their collections, stepped up the zest with which they hunted for the birds. The last great auk seen in British waters was off St Kilda. It was sighted in 1843, just one year before this magnificent bird went the same way as the dodo.

The great auk specimen in Torshavn Natural History Museum is only partly natural, being reconstructed from pieces of the real thing, plus parts from other birds.

We sailed around the southern side of the island of Vagar, where huge spires of rock fell into the sea. Perhaps the most impressive of these rock spires were the serrated pinnacles that formed a crest on the little island of Tindholmur. In a rough, choppy sea, we headed on towards the island of Mykines where we'd planned to land. By the time we were off shore from the village of Mykines, which is tucked into a delightful natural bay on the western side of the island, it was clear that we'd not be landing. Huge waves piled in onto the beach, and even as we sailed on, the ship was pitching wildly across her beam.

The headland of Mykinesholmur in the Faroes

From Mykines village a steep path would have led us over a grassy hill, then down into a deep cleft that lay between Mykines and Mykinesholmur. As we gazed across to this cleft, we could see a tiny footbridge that we would have crossed to get onto the island of Mykinesholmur.

The *Grigoriy Mikheev* rounded the northern side of the island, passing a pinnacle of rock coated with the guano from a few hundred nesting gannets, then continued into the lovely but wild bay of Viovik, on the northern side of Vagar. Here the seas were much calmer, and we enjoyed a superb Zodiac cruise around the bay. Massive walls of volcanic rock loomed over the tiny boats, but the skippers of each, Mick, Martin and Aleksandr, managed to give us an exhilarating ride into caves formed by basalt dykes and beneath a spectacular gushing waterfall where the Reipsa River drains the large lake of Fjallavatn on the moorland above. The river here has found a natural fault line, eroding the sides and making a superb force where the water pushes a way through the rock's imperfection, pouring a hundred feet or more into the broiling sea upon which our boats danced. The cliffs here backing the bay were immense, making the *Grigoriy Mikheev* look like a toy boat on a park pond.

After dinner, to celebrate what was by then pretty much 24 hours of daylight – what the Shetlanders would call 'simmer dim' – we went out again in the Zodiacs, this time round to the northern tip of Streymoy, where the huge fjord of Sundini cuts a vast channel between that island and Eysturoy.

On the shore there stands the tiny settlement of Tjørnuvik, well hidden at the head of a wonderful little bay. Going ashore here we floundered onto the slippery

Exploring the caves of the
Faroe Islands by Zodiac

pier, then watched as Arctic terns fished in the simmer dim, the glow of the sun still glancing off the calm waters of the cove. Oystercatchers displaying on the shingle beach reminded us that for many of these wading birds, their migration northwards was over. They'd settled on a piece of land upon which to nest that year and were getting on with the business of wooing their partner. Shags and black guillemots bobbed in the water, while a great northern diver flew purposefully overhead. Marsh marigolds, bright and cheery, starry saxifrage, showing tiny white flowers, and butterwort stars fringed the rocks where freshwater burns joined the salt water down on the shore. Sea sandwort filled the cracks among boulders that studded the volcanic grey-sand beach.

We walked around the settlement, admiring the crazily angled lazy-beds on the steep hillside as we ambled over to look at the Viking cemetery that lies up on the hill, overlooking Tjørnuvik.

Back on board I lay in my cabin as the deep rumble of the engines could be heard pushing us through the water towards Jan Mayen, our next destination. We were nearing the Arctic Circle and the far northern islands where we'd begin to see birds and mammals more typical of the tundra. In particular, I hoped to catch up with some of the birds that may have been on the Solway Firth during the winter – barnacle geese, whooper swans and waders.

The sun was still bright in the sky, even though it was nearly midnight, and we motored on into the dusk. I kept thinking back over the fate of the great auk. Wondering, among other things, why it had been given the Latin name *Pinguinus*.

A few weeks later, at home, I decided to do some research into this. Did the ornithologists of old think the great auk was just another species of penguin? Well, in a way, it seems that they did.

The original English name for the great auk was penguin – long before the penguins of the southern hemisphere were ever discovered – and the name became generally accepted among the seamen and explorers of the time. There are a number of islands off Newfoundland, one of the strongholds of the great auk, that still have the name Penguin Island today.

It is likely that when the Portuguese began exploring the coasts of South Africa and South America they would have come across other birds that very closely resembled the penguins of the north, what we now know as great auks. These newly discovered birds of the south were, quite naturally, called penguins too – they were large, black and white, flightless and swam swiftly through the water in search of fish. The name of these birds in the south has, as we are well aware, stayed with them, whereas the great auk's name changed, first from penguin to garefowl, then to great auk. We also now know that the great auk was not in any way related to the penguins of the south. The similarity between auks – and I include puffins, guillemots and razorbills – and penguins is what's known as convergent evolution. This is when animals that have evolved to live the same lifestyle tend to resemble each other, even though they are not related in any way, and may not even be from the same part of the world.

10

Crossing the Arctic Circle

A very foggy day dawned as we motored northwards towards the Arctic Circle and the island of Jan Mayen. There were a few birds following the ship: fulmars, kittiwakes, and gannets just tagging along for the ride. The first thing we noticed up on the monkey deck was a glowing fog-bow off the port bow. This phenomenon is a little like the Brocken spectres I'd seen on Scottish mountains. It occurs when particles of mist or spray act like a million tiny prisms, with the sun filtering through them from behind an object, in this case the *Grigoriy Mikheev*. We all watched with glee at the rare sight of a large white arc following the ship northwards towards the Arctic Circle.

Our guides entertained us with occasional talks or slide-show presentations, and on this long sea-day, Mick gave an introduction to the birds of the North Atlantic, illustrated by a fine selection of slides taken over a number of years. Martin followed this with sketches of whales and other cetaceans, explaining how we could identify them from a distance. We all crammed into the lecture theatre – erstwhile the dining room – for these talks, and they often proved to be really informative, as well as good fun.

That night I enjoyed a good sleep. We passed over the Arctic Circle at about 3 a.m, though I didn't wake to witness it, unlike some of the other passengers. I'm not sure that any of them felt the slight 'bump' that Martin had promised, as the ship passed over the line, but they did raise a glass with the watch on the bridge. We were now in the Arctic summer and were enjoying a full 24 hours of daylight, if not sunshine. The dense fog bank that had shrouded the ship all through the previous day, projecting the spectacular fog-bow across our bows, still hadn't lifted, although visibility was marginally better.

More fulmars passed the ship, all heading north now, although no other birds were present. I kept wondering when we'd start to see the dark phase or blue fulmar, as they are more common the further north you go, but so far it had been just the pale-phase birds that we are familiar with in Britain that were circling us.

The sea was getting a little choppier by then but was still relatively calm, and the *Grigoriy Mikheev* had taken on a very gentle side-to-side roll as she carried on the swell from the south-west.

Another of Mick's presentations took place that afternoon. This one was about the role of timepieces and chronometers in sea navigation. Mick seems to be a very genuine and level-headed chap. Originally from Dublin, and now living on the Pembrokeshire coast, he is obviously passionate about wildlife, with seabirds as his specialism, and gannets in particular. That afternoon's talk on the history of navigation at sea gave us a taste of one of his other passions, that of timepieces, and it was again fascinating and great fun.

As we continued northwards for Jan Mayen, we were joined by a couple of stowaways. An adult lesser black-backed gull circled the ship a couple of times, then came on board, landing on the forward deck in among where the Zodiacs were stored. Within a few minutes another – this one a much younger subadult, still speckled and pathetic-looking – came and stood in the bows, hunched up and looking very sorry for itself. They pretty much ignored each other for an hour or so, the youngster sulking as teenagers tend to do, while the adult strode brightly around the deck. Then the adult spotted something floating on the sea and swooped down to collect it. It looked like a piece of cardboard, or possibly birch bark, and the adult carefully seized it from the gentle swell. He flew in a couple of huge arcs across the sky, squawking triumphantly. Finally, it brought its prize back to the ship and with great poise landed delicately on the gunwale. The youngster, which was probably the adult's chick from the previous year, thought it might be dinner time and went over to its parent, mewing softly and submissively at the older bird. The adult took great exception to this, going berserk at the very thought of sharing his piece of cardboard with this young upstart. He swung at the youngster, knocking it over onto the deck, and then chased it out over the sea.

The few spectators up on the monkey deck – remember this was now our second consecutive full day at sea, and, bearing in mind that we'd had no visibility for most of this time, most of the passengers had by now retreated either to the bar, the bridge or their own cabins – obviously thought the fledgling was a goner. However, once the lesson was learned, the adult flew back in, still with his piece of cardboard clamped firmly in his bill, and alighted back on the deck. The youngster – perhaps it wasn't the chick of the adult after all – came back in looking truly exhausted and collapsed.

They both remained with us for the rest of the day but had gone by the morning, presumably continuing to Jan Mayen under their own steam.

At 5 p.m., there came an announcement over the tannoy – 'Whale off the port side.' We all swung up on deck as the ship turned sharply about and came to a halt in its own swell. Martin had spotted the whale from the bridge and announced that it was a minke. He'd decided that there really wasn't much point in us hanging around, as the whale had seemed to be moving quickly southwards. He had just given the captain the go ahead to return to our course for Jan Mayen, when Ann-Marie, one of the passengers, spotted a blow dead ahead. Then there was another and another. Minke whales don't blow, and besides, these were brown in colour whereas minkes are black.

The *Grigoriy Mikheev* lay at rest, motionless on the water. Two more bushy blows and a good view of the tell-tale coloration of northern bottlenose whales, light brown as they broke the surface just off the port bow.

Way out to the west, someone again spotted the minke, causing a crest in the meniscus of the ocean surface as it eased upwards with its back. Then that giant of the seas was gone, diving deep.

The bottlenose whales surfaced another five times, allowing good views, but only two animals at a time. However, there could easily have been more. They moved away to the north-west, breaking the surface every now and again, and we left them to it as we resumed our course directly for Jan Mayen.

The northern bottlenose whale is one of the larger members of the beaked whale family. As with other members of this family, this species has very few teeth. They are happiest in the deeper sections of the ocean and can stay under for over an hour at a time. The deepest a northern bottlenose whale has been recorded is nearly 1,500 metres! They occur throughout the North Atlantic, from the coast of Maine northwards on the west side to the UK northwards on the east, and they congregate in what is known as The Gully, off the coast of Nova Scotia each April to calve.

The following morning we were approaching the remote island of Jan Mayen. We'd had two full days heading through the Norwegian Sea and had been embroiled in a dense sea fog the whole time. The ocean currents carried a swell from the south, making it difficult for us to even contemplate going ashore on that side of the island. Martin had spoken to the station commander on Jan Mayen, and he'd suggested that we sail on around the sheltered north side and attempt a landing there.

Jan Mayen is a lonely island, lying 200-odd miles from the east coast of Greenland, and 300 miles north from Iceland. The first discoverers of the island are unknown, although it is known that St Brendan travelled these waters in the years around AD 489–580. Along with his band of monkish followers, he probably came across Jan Mayen, as well as Greenland, and some believe possibly America.

Some also think it possible that the Vikings found Jan Mayen on their voyages to Greenland some 400–600 years later, although there have been no archaeological remains from either civilisation found on Jan Mayen itself.

Next came the Venetian explorer, Nicolo Zeno, who ventured out on expeditions in these waters from 1390 until 1405. Although the sketches he made in his log were far from accurate, on a sketch map of the region he clearly marked a large volcano some way north of Iceland and east of Greenland. In Zeno's diary he makes mention of seeing monks using hot springs for heating and also using kayaks for hunting. On the south-eastern side of Jan Mayen, at a place named Ekroldalen, there are what are believed to be the ruins of a settlement and an artificial irrigation system. A female skull has also been found here, so it does seem at least plausible that Jan Mayen is the place Zeno documented.

Henry Hudson came across Jan Mayen in 1607, and Thomas Marmaduke visited five years later. However, it was an Englishman who made the first documented landing on Jan Mayen. John Clarke saw the island three times in 1614 and went ashore to collect walrus. He named the island 'Isabella'. Three other ships also called in at Jan Mayen that same year, all of them Dutch. One was captained by Jan Jacobs May, after whom Jan Mayen was eventually named.

The Dutch pretty much made Jan Mayen their own in the early years as they made regular hunting forays to the island. In 1614, the Noordsche Compagnie was formed as a whaling company, and the Dutch withdrew their interests in Svalbard as a whaling base. This, however, was remarkably short-lived. Although heavy catches were common in the early years, by 1642 all the Jan Mayen stations were being closed down. The whale stocks were getting low throughout the waters of both Jan Mayen and Svalbard, and the various national fleets had to travel further and further afield to hunt.

We rounded the southern tip of the island in the thick fog. Then, as we coasted along the Sør Jan – the south-western peninsula of Jan Mayen – the dense cloak slowly began to lift. Great mountain ridges were revealed, thrown up from the sea, many of them snow-capped. We passed the tranquil bay of Sjuhollenderbukta, the place where the entire crew of a Dutch company died in the winter of 1633/34. They were attempting to overwinter on this desolate island, and they all died of scurvy.

Kvalrossbukta on the north-west side of Jan Mayen was our destination for the morning. We motored along this impressive west coast of the island, then as the mist cleared further, dead ahead, rising like Mount Fiji, stood the white volcanic dome of Beerenberg. This huge mass of mountain drew us into the sheltered bay at Kvalrossbukta (which means, simply, walrus bay), and we all went ashore in the Zodiacs.

We were met on the rocky shore by the station commander, who welcomed us warmly. He was a burly chap who managed to look both delighted to see us, and slightly uncomfortable having to greet 20-odd strangers to his shores. Ours was the first ship to call in at Jan Mayen that season, which meant that apart from the other Norwegian scientists based on Jan Mayen, we were the first outsiders they'd seen for about eight months. He told us that two supply ships were due to call in

Whale bones on the beach on Jan Mayen

later that month, and with good weather the odd plane would be sent out from Norway with new staff. He took our passports and sped off in his four-wheel drive truck, crossing the island via its narrow isthmus.

The beach at Kvalrossbukta was littered with the flotsam of hundreds of years of whaling – huge bones of fin, sperm and northern bottle-nosed whales jutting out of the sand, each bone bleached white by the sun and scoured by the relentless wind. The sand itself was black and ashen, thrust from the volcanic dome of Beerenberg, setting off the bleak starkness of the landscape, while grass-covered scree slopes, vividly green in the clean light, seemed to flow in long ribs from the low hills above the bay.

We split into two groups, and I went with Mick along the track towards the Norwegian Meteorological Station. This took us along the track over the isthmus, in a six-mile hike over the grey, ashy remains of the volcanic interior. Dark clouds shrouded our little group as we climbed above the bay at Kvalrossbukta, crossing a low col. The flanks above the col to the north, just a little rocky lump of red stone, liberally coated with Arctic sedges, hid one of the birds I'd been desperate to see on this trip. We stopped for a while and listened hard as the clouds parted then drew closed again. As they parted a second time, a small flock of birds, nothing more than a vague black-and-white fluttering, passed overhead and vanished, blending into the rocky slope on which they'd just landed. I scanned over the slope and immediately picked out a few puffins with my binoculars, and then as Mick

Exploring the island of Jan Mayen

explained that this slope is one of the nesting colonies of the little auk, I began to see these tiny birds too.

They are the smallest members of the auk family – no bigger than a starling and are one of the classic species of the Arctic. We were really struggling to see these delightful birds well, but Mick thought we might see them much closer once we got up to Svalbard. Over the wind there carried an occasional 'kree-ak ak ak ak', the wonderful sound made by the little auk when it is busy about its nesting site.

The narrow neck of land we were crossing effectively forms a central belt to the two halves of the island of Jan Mayen. Our route led from the north-west side at Kvalrossbukta to the southern side where the Met Station is based at Olonkinbyen, along with the tiny air-landing strip.

Crossing the isthmus our views were limited by the persistent cloud. It did peel apart on the odd occasion, revealing an enormous stretch of black-sand beach reaching along the north shore towards Beerenberg. As we reached the highest point of the track, and began the short descent to the south shore, more and more was revealed. A vast expanse of water filled a trough on the beach – the Sørlaguna backed by huge piles of driftwood. Glaucous gulls and Arctic terns nested down by the shore, while Arctic skuas chased everything in sight, desperate for a free meal. Down on the dark shore ringed and golden plovers, and a handful of red knot picked along the line of the surf.

Jagged crenellations of rock, pushed up during the volcanic island's turbulent past, cut the clouds above us as we walked along the track which ran parallel to the Sørlaguna. We arrived in dribs and drabs at the Meteorological Station,

Left: Traffic warning signs on Jan Mayen

Below: Timber from Siberian logging camps on a beach on Jan Mayen

passing a few other huts on the walk in. We were welcomed to the station by the commander and his staff, who busied around making us tea and coffee. A film was shown depicting the human history of Jan Mayen, and also the life on the island today.

Afterwards I wandered alone, following the shoreline back towards the isthmus, spotting lots of waders and kittiwakes. The clouds now hung in a thick layer around the base of the mountains, while their summits pierced a clear blue sky. As I dodged the surf breaking onto the sandy beach, Beerenberg loomed ahead and looked magnificent.

About 380 square kilometres of volcano lie above the waterline on Jan Mayen, and Beerenberg is the highest point of this. At 2,277 metres above the sea, this snow-covered dome dominates the north side of the island, Nord-Jan. The volcanic activity that has created Jan Mayen occurred on the seabed, and the crater rim of Beerenberg, upon which lies the highest point, is actually 5,000 metres above the ocean floor.

Back on board the *Grigoriy Mikheev*, we sailed around the northern tip of Jan Mayen where we could get the best views of the great glaciers edging down from the crater rim of Beerenberg. I went onto the main deck with Martin at one point to watch hundreds of thousands of Brunnich's guillemots and little auks bobbing around on the sea and filling the cliffs above.

Below: Beerenberg, Jan Mayen's volcano

The evening turned very cold as we put our stern to Jan Mayen and its mighty Beerenberg and steamed away towards the compact form of Bear Island, anchored out of sight over miles of ocean somewhere between the Greenland Sea and the Barents Sea.

Beerenberg Glacier on Jan Mayen

11

Bear Island

Bjørnøya, often known by its Anglicised name, Bear Island, lies in the middle of the Barents Sea, about halfway between the northern tip of mainland Europe, Nord Kapp, and the southern tip of Svalbard.

The island is known to many English-speaking people as the setting for one of Alistair MacLean's thrillers, which goes by the same name. The book was first published in 1971, and a feature film followed in 1980, although most of the shooting was done in Alaska and Canada where the scenery does not at all resemble that on the real island.

The story, at least in the novel, follows the fate of a converted fishing trawler, the *Morning Rose*, as she crosses the Barents Sea with a film-making crew on board. They are heading for Bear Island to make a movie, although only the producer and screenwriter know the exact plot that the film will eventually take. Perhaps predictably, on the crossing to Bear Island, certain members of the film-crew, along with a few of the ship's crew, die in mysterious circumstances. The hero, Marlowe, who is the doctor on board, finds himself at the centre of a plot where it turns out that few of the passengers are who they claim to be. The murders continue once they are on Bear Island, and Marlowe, who is also not who he claims to be, has to unravel it all and discovers that the whole thing is intertwined with forgotten events of the Second World War.

The film was greatly different in plot to the novel, although it did introduce viewers to Bjørnøya, even if only by name.

On board the *Grigoriy Mikheev* Martin gave all passengers a safety briefing as we were now nearing Bear Island. From now on wherever we went ashore on any of the islands of the Svalbard group we had to be accompanied by either Martin or Mick who would carry guns and flares to deter any polar bears that we might encounter. Martin pointed out that it was unlikely that we'd see polar bears on Bear Island itself, but that some do get caught there during occasional summers.

*

Wild and remote in the Barents Sea, the island of Bjørnøya

Polar bears walk south across the drift-ice during the winter – one bear was shot during the first discovery of the island by Barents in 1596 – and then retreat northwards with the ice during the thaw. Any bears that do remain on the island soon become crazed with hunger. During the summer of 2004 a female bear with two cubs that were too weak to swim became trapped on Bear Island, and, back in the summer of 1971, a crew member, Bjørn Tessen, working at the weather station on the island, was attacked by a bear just 50 metres from his hut.

It is assumed that about 100 of these great ice bears make it down to Bjørnøya each winter, or at least they have until very recent times. As our sea temperatures rise with global warming, there is less and less pack ice forming, and it may not be too long before *Ursus maritimus*, the polar bear, retreats further and further north, or even dies out altogether.

We approached Bjørnøya over a grey sea, enjoying the spectacle of three sperm whales rising very close to our bows. Seabirds were everywhere, indicating that we were approaching land, and hundreds of Brunnich's guillemots, little auks, puffins, kittiwakes and glaucous gulls headed towards our destination.

The glaucous gulls were good to see, being largely unfamiliar to most of us in Britain. They are a very large gull and can be identified by a pure white body and grey wing-tops. There is no black on a glaucous gull, which all the species you're likely to find in Britain have, either on their backs, heads or wing-tips.

A sperm whale dives in the Greenland Sea

Also great to spot were the fulmars. Anyone who has walked around a coastal headland in Britain will have seen these superb soaring birds as they fly by stiff-winged, but here in the Arctic they appeared different to those I'd seen back at home.

Fulmars have a number of distinct colour phases – those around Britain are generally pure white but with slatey-grey backs and wings. Here, as we approached Bjørnøya, more and more of them seemed to be a kind of dusky blue-grey all over, and Mick pointed out that this was a sure sign that we were reaching higher latitudes.

By late afternoon we were within sight of the mighty cliffs of Bjørnøya. Hundreds of thousands of birds peeled off the cliffs like swarms of bees.

We headed up the east coast of the island, passing immense coastal cliffs topped by rounded, snow-flecked summits, and finally dropped anchor in a secluded bay as the late evening light paled slightly to the cold, grey colour of the sea.

I went up onto the monkey deck in the chill of the night. An open cove backed by lush tundra growth lay to the west, the gateway to its back being formed by jagged pinnacles of rock rent by fault lines and caves. Blue fulmar petrels scythed the air around my head, while a mash of guillemots, little auks and a few puffins dotted the cold sea below me.

I turned in that night excited about the prospect of setting foot on this wild and remote island where nature rules, and the weather is king.

Early the following morning we stepped ashore from the Zodiacs at a stony beach. This was the cove I had looked into last night, and to gain the shore we'd cut through the waters that lay between the rocky entrance to the bay. This was Kvalrossbukta, named in the same way as its namesake on Jan Mayen, after the fact that it used to be a walrus-hunting station.

English whalers came to Bjørnøya first, in 1604, seven years before whaling began elsewhere in Svalbard. They also took huge numbers of walrus for blubber and ivory, and recorded a bag of 600 walrus in a day. These walrus hunts became less productive as numbers dwindled, although in the 18th century the Russians followed the English to the island and caught seals, walrus and foxes, as well as collecting eggs and down from the large colonies of birds. Occasional polar bears were taken too.

At Kvalrossbukta we found the stark remains of the most recent whaling station. Here whales were processed between 1905 and 1909, and all that we could find, apart from a huge boiler that still balanced on an old wooden frame, were the sites of one or two buildings, now long gone, and a jumble of wooden struts and wire cables.

We split into two groups, Martin leading half the group on an exploration of the valley floor, while I joined Mick on a walk up into the mountains. We climbed above the bay as a huge flock of kittiwakes rose off the tundra in front of us.

Mosses covered the slopes, right down to the gurgling stream in the base of the corrie, and waders picked over the ground, moving ahead of us as we approached. Eight pink-footed geese broke into the air, flying in a large arc around the rim of the corrie, and then coming in to rest on the flanks of the northern hill.

Purple sandpipers were everywhere, while turnstones looked gorgeous in their summer breeding plumage. We climbed to a point overlooking a bay to the south of Kvalrossbukta, and far below us, we caught sight of a young bearded seal rolling playfully in the surf.

On we climbed, slowly gaining height as the cloud capping the hilltops descended to greet us. We were soon right beneath the cloud base, and Mick seemed unhappy about continuing. He pointed out that although the chance of coming across a polar bear was very slim, he didn't want to risk it in the bad visibility, and so we turned tail and dropped back into the valley above Kvalrossbukta.

I asked if he'd mind if I walked a few yards away on the seaward side, parallel to the group, so that I could photograph the sandpipers and turnstones. He thought this would be fine, as the rest of the group would be between the main landmass and me, and as I'd only be a short distance away anyway, he was sure I wouldn't be at risk from any polar bears.

I moved off over the tundra, glad to be even a few feet away from the confines of the group. Photographing purple sandpipers on their summer breeding grounds was something I'd always wanted to do. I managed to snap off half a dozen shots and kept close to the group as they moved across the floor of the corrie towards Martin's group. A white wagtail dipped from stone to stone in the slowly moving stream as it pushed gently through the dense carpet of mosses, and a pair of turnstones flew in to a few feet of where I walked.

I heard Mick's radio crackle and could make out a stream of invective from Martin. He obviously thought I was just wandering off on my own and was very concerned about the bear risk. I could hear this easily and within a minute I was back with the group and apologised to Mick for putting him in an awkward situation.

We met up with Martin's group at a point where the stream cut down a small rocky gorge from the plateau above. I had a quick word with Martin, too, and apologised for leaving the group. His little band were very pleased with themselves as soon after we'd left them an Arctic fox had come down from the fells to the north, sniffed briefly around our life jackets that we'd left by the boiler at Kvalrossbukta, then walked bravely up to his astonished group. They had sat and watched him for 20 minutes or so, and Martin had even been able to reach out and let the little grey fox sniff his hand.

Purple saxifrages flowered on the gravel ground, and a cock snow bunting picked for seeds among the grit. The eight pink-footed geese came wheeling in again, over our heads, landing briefly, then took off into the intense low cloud for a destination somewhere west of our little corrie.

Had this been a little later in the year, during the southward migration, there would undoubtedly have been thousands of barnacle geese here on Bjørnøya too. Indeed, this vast mossy plateau land upon which Mick had led us on our short excursion would have been heavily grazed for a few short weeks by hungry geese, all feeding up prior to the flight down to the Solway Firth. It was here, during September later that year, that Barbow, the record-breaking barnacle goose, would spend a fortnight before turning a course southwards for the coast of Norway, on his way to the Solway wintering grounds – a destination that that particular goose would never reach.

Back on board ship we enjoyed a quick snack lunch before heading out again in the Zodiacs for a cruise along the west coast. Suddenly we were right down at water level with millions of seabirds – guillemots flapped wildly in great clouds, while others dived below the surface. A flotilla of eider ducks bobbed in a small cove, and a magnificent king eider, a true bird of the north, flew in with a handful of the more common individuals and landed among the throng.

In a small voe to the north we spotted a tiny wooden hut, and Martin, who was at the helm of the Zodiac I was in, decided to go ashore to have a look. Glaucous gulls sat on nests around the weathered building, while more eiders swam along the shore as we landed on a pebbly beach.

The hut looked as though it was slowly becoming part of this wild landscape. Its weather-beaten walls had lost much of their paint in long flakes and chips, revealing grey, knotted wood beneath, and we had a quick look inside. A couple of bunks, a gas stove, settle, axes and saws, pots, pans and water bottles were stored neatly within its dark interior.

I tried to imagine what the trapper who lived here during the season must be like. Obviously a gnarled, hardy character, used to a life in one of the most inhospitable, remote corners of the world. One of the walls outside had four large rents across the greying grain. These looked fairly fresh and had to be from some large animal trying to break into the hut for food. Polar bear, thought Martin. I hoped the food the bear had sniffed out was not the trapper himself!

Back in the Zodiacs we skimmed along the surface of the quiet coves and headed back towards the ship as a hard, cold wind got up and drove sleet into our faces.

Just one thing remained to be done before we headed north and left Bjørnøya behind for ever. Captain Aleksandr had been asked by the Norwegian staff on Jan Mayen to deliver a letter to the staff at the radio station and survey base on Bjørnøya.

At the end of the Second World War, a temporary building was erected at the northern end of Bjørnøya at a place called Tunheim. This was the site of an old coal-mining settlement on the island, and the new building housed what became Bjørnøya Radio. The station is still very active and serves as a weather station, too, providing vital information to marine and air navigators.

The *Grigoriy Mikheev* anchored offshore within the sight of the small Norwegian base, while the captain took a Zodiac ashore to deliver the letter. He was probably the first outsider the staff there had seen since the last summer season, and we watched through binoculars as he stepped ashore, shook hands solemnly with the four or five people who had gone down to the shore to greet him, handed over the letter, then returned to the ship and set a course for Svalbard. We wondered just what important message the letter might have contained, that our captain had been specially commissioned with the job of delivering it in person. Most likely it was just a postcard from Jan Mayen!

12

Summering in Svalbard

In 1596, one of the greatest of the world's early explorers, the Dutchman Willem Barents, was commissioned as chief pilot with a small expedition heading up into Arctic waters. Barents' aim was that of trying to search for and establish the North-east Passage to the Orient. Barents had attempted to find a way to the Far East through the waters of Arctic Russia in both 1594 and 1595, but both expeditions had failed to find the route through. In 1956, his crew were heading north when, on 9 June, they spotted the island of Bjørnøya. Moving on from there they discovered the Svalbard archipelago, naming the land they saw Spitsbergen, which means 'pointed mountains' in Dutch. Continuing in their search for a North-east Passage the explorers came across Novaya Zemlya where the advancing winter caused them to camp for the season. The crew suffered greatly from the harsh weather and intense cold, and on 20 June 1597, Barents himself died before the party could get him to safety.

So, what's in a name? Svalbard or Spitsbergen? Well, the archipelago seems to go under both names. Although Barents is credited with discovering the island group in 1596, the old Icelandic Annals of 1194 have a passage which talks of a place called Svalbard, which means 'cold coast'. However, there is no firm evidence to suggest that this particular 'cold coast' is the same as Barents' later discovery. Now that Svalbard is in Norwegian hands, they prefer to use the old Viking name, in recognition of the possible Viking discovery, rather than that given by the Dutchman, and so Svalbard is now the group's official name. However, and rather confusingly, the biggest island of the Svalbard group is called Spitsbergen.

Our group of modern-day explorers settled in for a final night on passage to the Svalbard archipelago.

Sunshine filtering through the porthole of my cabin awakened me at the ungodly hour of 4 a.m. I sat on the couch by the window for a while, feeling the by now very familiar gentle tilt and turn of the swell against the hull of the *Grigoriy Mikheev*. A cold-looking dawn sky filled the horizon, speckled by flitting kittiwakes and the odd glaucous gull. I read for a while, showered, dressed warmly in my layers of Paramo clothing, and then went up on deck to see if we had sight of any land. All around us open sea stretched to the horizon, with not a dot of land anywhere. I went back to my cabin, stripped off my outer layers, dumped the camera and binoculars on the bed, then went down for breakfast.

I sat with Roger and Caroline, a middle-aged couple from Yorkshire who now live in the Chilterns, and we chatted about the birds we'd seen so far during the trip. The sun pushed through the glass and around the paint drips on the portholes of the dining room as we talked, and we excitedly kept glancing out to see if we could yet see Svalbard. Just as we were finishing, washing down a last cup of strong coffee, a large flock of little auks dashed by the porthole nearest to our table. A whizzing of wings, black and white flashing against the bright light, and then they were gone. We all shot off to prepare ourselves for the -10 temperatures out on deck and soon huddled together with the other passengers on the monkey deck.

The most immediate and obvious thing we saw were the small blocks of sea ice through which we were now passing. This was all very exciting – for this was the very first of the Arctic pack ice we'd encountered during the trip.

I'd talked to both Martin and Mick about the pack ice we expected to come across. Both had told me that in years past they would have expected to have hit the sea ice at this early point in the summer season either around the shores of Bjørnøya or very soon thereafter. Mick in particular seemed very worried about the obvious signs of global warming at hand in the Arctic.

As we motored northwards in thicker and thicker ice, more and more birds studded the floes or flew by the ship in strings. Little auks were now all around us, and as I followed a group of these wonderful little black-and-white flecks across the seascape with my binoculars, I suddenly found the far distant views being filled with snow-capped mountains, each peak riven by dark gullies of shale. Svalbard!

Captain Aleksandr was slowly and steadily nosing the *Grigoriy Mikheev* northwards into the wide seaway known as Storfjorden. This channel, 30 to 40 miles wide, separates the islands of Spitsbergen, the main and most westerly of the bigger islands of the archipelago, from the islands of Edgeøya and Barentsøya. The land I could see in the distance was the Kvalpyntfonna Mountains of Edgeøya. We weren't heading for Edgeøya, however, simply passing by it at a great distance as we explored the ice floes of the Storfjorden.

Out on some of these floes, dark shapes looked back at us – bearded and harp seals basking in the sunshine, their bellies so well insulated by blubber and fur that they didn't melt the ice on which they rested.

More and more little auks filed past and were occasionally followed closely by great and Arctic skuas, intent on finding a meal. I was observing a couple of glaucous gulls, huge birds on the wing as they swung by the ship, when suddenly Caroline shouted me over to the front of the monkey deck where she'd been watching a blue-phase fulmar scything across the frozen wastes. From the railings overlooking the bow she pointed down off the port side at one of the small bergs of ice.

'Look. Footprints!' She cried excitedly at the small crowd that had gathered.

We all gazed down at a line of four very large prints in the soft snow that had settled on top of the ice floe. There was no doubt at all – these were the relatively fresh prints of a polar bear, the first signs we had seen so far of the presence of this great ice bear in the pack ice.

Polar bears, or ice bears as they are also known, are the largest bear species in the world, and a healthy male can weigh in at an impressive 700 kg. Such a huge mass of predatory muscle plays a very important role in the ecosystem of the Arctic, and indeed polar bears are the world's largest living land carnivore. The carcasses of their kills provide a vital food source for other species, such as the Arctic fox, the glaucous gull and the ivory gull.

They vary in colour from off-white through cream to yellow, and can also be grey. These great ice bears are so well insulated beneath their thick pelage of creamy white fur that they are practically invisible to a heat sensor.

Sea ice seems to be vital to the existence of polar bears – although they have a circumpolar distribution, covering the entire Arctic, they are by and large restricted to areas which are covered in sea ice for a significant part of the year. This enables them to cover large distances and to hunt for seals in blow-holes formed in the ice.

The 20,000 to 25,000 polar bears thought to be present in the Arctic today, according to figures released by the World Conservation Monitoring Centre in Cambridge, are divided into 19 distinct populations, known as 'stocks'. These stocks range from Alaska, through Canada to Greenland, across the whole of the Russian Arctic and into the Norwegian Arctic. It is possible to find polar bears as far south as James Bay in Canada, at 50°N, and as far north as the North Pole itself. Occasionally bears have made it as far south as Iceland, simply by walking over the frozen seas of the Arctic winter.

Surprisingly, their numbers are actually stable at present and have been since the 1980s. Prior to that there had been a minor population explosion, bringing the world figures up from about 10,000 bears in 1965 to around 20,000 in 1983.

However, the future is not at all bright for the polar bear, and a recent review of the status of polar bears has concluded that there is likely to be an overall decline of more than 30 per cent within the next 35 to 50 years. The principal cause of this projected decline is global warming and its consequent negative effects on the vital sea ice on which the bears rely.

I scanned around slowly with my binoculars, first swinging clockwise from the bow and going full circle around the ship, then going back widdershins, scanning for even a small glimpse of a bear. Nothing at all, other than more birds passing by. The other thing I did notice was that there was now land away to the north and west too – these were the mountains of the Torrell Land and Heer Land regions of Spitsbergen, which were a good 10 miles or so away. The foreground was filled with pack-ice soup – just soggy looking drifts through which you simply couldn't imagine a bear wanting to travel. I suppose this was actually a prime hunting ground for polar bears, there being a good supply of food out here on the floes, with countless birds roosting on bergs and seals hauled out on the larger blocks.

Martin came up onto the monkey deck and told us to keep our eyes open for bears – he seemed unimpressed by our sightings of bear prints in the snow and said that we'd see a lot more of those before the day was out. He also said that the plan for the day was that we'd motor on into the pack ice until we could find a good place for lunch. It seemed that there'd be some kind of barbeque on the afterdeck; the engines would be cut so that the entire crew could join us for lunch. I gazed around over the endless miles of frozen water, wondering exactly what you looked for when choosing a good lunch spot in the middle of all this ice.

Then, as Martin went down to the bridge to talk his plans through with the captain, Mick came over the tannoy, excitedly telling all on deck that there had been a sighting of a polar bear. We all followed his directions with our binoculars, way out over the ice-lump flats off the port bow. About a mile or so away, amid the shimmering spikes and towers of pure white ice, we could see a creamy figure ambling along towards us. Martin took over on the tannoy and explained that we were going to take the ship a little closer, but not so close as to frighten the bear.

The captain turned slowly to the port side, crunching the bows through thick chunks of drift ice. The whole ship shuddered as it pushed some lumps to the sides, each piece of ice scouring the paint off the hull at sea level. The bigger bergs, some perhaps 50 or 60 feet across, but each not more than perhaps 10 feet high above the dark waters, broke as the bow nosed onto them.

The great ice bear heard the crunch of metal against ice, and the grumbling of the ship's engines carrying across the Arctic seascape, and stopped atop a crown of ice. He turned towards the *Grigoriy Mikheev* and stared. We eased gently forwards, towards the bear, then as it began moving again, this time on a diagonal course that would have taken it around our stern, the captain cut the engines and all was silent. So silent, we could hear the ice crunching under the bear's huge pads as it again altered course and this time came straight towards the ship.

The silence was beautiful, and at last I was able to feel that this was the true Arctic, the furthest reaches of the Earth. Wilderness surrounded us, and wildness was right off our port beam in the form of a large male polar bear. He was now perhaps 500 yards away, and we all crammed around the rails of the monkey deck and side decks, cameras clicking away.

Male polar bear hunting on ice floes in Storfjorden

The bear strode purposefully closer, obviously sniffing the air, then turned in a circle, coming at first closer still, then veering off to cross the ship's bows not more than 70 yards away. At one point he broke through the thin film of ice that covered the dark waters of the Storfjorden. He clambered easily out the other side of the break and onto firmer ice, then carried on regardless as if nothing had happened, very obviously at home in this wild place, his natural environment. As he crossed our bows I had a thought – we were all up on the monkey deck clicking away with our cameras, but the point of the bow itself was perhaps 20 yards from the superstructure where we were perched. If I ran down right to the very tip of the bow itself before he passed by I'd get some very close pictures of my first wild polar bear.

I dashed down the various decks of the ship and out onto the bows, noticing that six or seven of the other passengers had followed me. As I took up position with my camera, I saw Mick was next to me, and we both laughed as we clicked away. Angel, the ship's hotel manager was close by, also snapping away – it seemed that even these old hands of the Arctic were thoroughly enjoying the spectacle of the bear passing so close.

The bear itself moved off, towards a large drift of pack ice where a couple of dozen gulls roosted. As he moved away Martin's voice carried over the ice plains from the tannoy, announcing that lunch was being served on the afterdeck.

So now, after three hours of crashing through the loosely packed sea ice of the Storfjorden the MV *Grigoriy Mikheev* now floated at rest, engines silent, going gently with the flow of the channel as all its crew and passengers enjoyed a bizarre barbecue on the rear deck. The stunning glacial mountains of Torrell Land on the east coast of the island of Spitsbergen now filled the horizon, pale yellow sun reflecting off the snow, the sky a strange violet-blue. Nearer at hand the large glaucous gulls crowded about the ship, perching on icebergs and chasing each other through the vivid cobalt skies of the Arctic summer.

It was a surreal moment, for as we each tucked into the superb food – chicken legs, pork chops, sausages, burgers, rice, pasta and fresh salad – washing it down with mulled wine and cheap lager, tinny Russian pop music carried across the barren wastes from the small stereo that the crew had brought to the party.

Two of the girls – one of the chefs and one of the Turkish cabin girls – bravely entertained us with a bizarre Turkish belly dance. The passengers and the rest of the crew huddled beneath piles of down clothing, thick woolly hats and gloves, thermal underwear and countless fleecy mid-layers, while these two beauties twirled and shook their booties and bellies. They were dressed in traditional costume – nothing more than bra and pants covered by provocatively draped layers of bright silk. Their bare feet stamped out the beat to the quirky pop music, jewellery jangled and sparkled with the ice-reflected light, and we all laughed and joined in.

Less than 100 yards from the ship, draped atop a large island of ice, the huge polar bear snoozed the afternoon away. He'd doubled back to the ship, presumably with the whiff of cooking meat in his keen nostrils. He seemed very inquisitive and soon realised that all the action was happening at the back end of the ship. He came very close, sniffing the air avidly, then climbed to the top of his ice island from where he could get a good view of the strange human cargo of the ship, and then lay down and, amid the noise of chatter and laughing, went to sleep. I had no doubt that once the party was over and we'd moved off, he'd come over to the ship-shaped break in the ice floe to check for scraps that the crew may have left for him.

Strangely, after a few glasses of mulled wine, I began to feel a little sea sick. We'd been through a bit of rough weather during our voyage, although admittedly nowhere near as bad as I'd expected, and I'd felt fine the whole time. Now, as we floated on the ice with the engines at rest, I felt decidedly queasy for the first time. I escaped the party and went up onto the top deck for a while, then settled in my cabin for a short nap.

An hour or so later, I awoke to the familiar sound of the engines. I dressed and went up on deck, feeling much better for my short sleep. The party was over and we had begun to move away from our lunch spot. The captain turned the ship to the west and motored in through thick ice towards Torrell Land. Loud crashing noises accompanied our progress, and more and more birds flew in towards the land.

Brunnich's guillemots passed by in their thousands, as did little auks. Kittiwakes called shrilly over the noise of the engines and glaucous gulls followed in our wake.

I went down to the stern to see if the polar bear was still there, perhaps picking among our scraps. I was very much in two minds as to whether or not I'd be happier if the crew had left him anything. On the one hand, the bear could no doubt do with any supplementary food he could find, yet on the other, surely dumping our waste, even a small amount, in the frozen wastes of the Arctic could not be a good thing. With hindsight, I sincerely hope that the crew didn't leave anything for the bear, however tempting it might have been.

I have the same issues when I'm taking groups out walking in the Highlands of Scotland – we go into these areas to appreciate the wildness and beauty, and it really would seem like sacrilege to despoil it by leaving anything behind that doesn't belong there.

The bear was nowhere to be seen, so perhaps he'd been fed up with waiting for the party to end and had wandered off to hunt for food of his own accord.

Mick joined me at the stern, and we marvelled at the vivid colours of the sky – the cold violet-blue of earlier that afternoon had intensified and now ranged from a deep cobalt through waxy purple to pale violet from one horizon to the other. Set against this icy array of cold hues, kittiwakes and glaucous gulls stood out starkly, looking whiter than I'd ever seen them before. And here, floating behind the ship as we retreated from the Storfjorden, was another species of gull, and one I'd never seen before.

'Ivory gulls,' Mike told me. 'Look at how white they are. No other colours or shades, not even grey, except a very pale yellow bill, a beady black eye and black legs.'

We prepared our cameras and took a dozen or more shots each of these wonderful little gulls of the Arctic. One or two dropped onto icebergs by the side of the ship and as they landed, they immediately vanished – blending into their surroundings so well that even as we watched them land we simply could not see them anymore. Ivory gulls are purely Arctic. They spend the entire year – both the breeding season and the very long, harsh and dark winters – above the 70°N latitude line.

This had certainly been an action-packed day, especially when you consider that we'd not set foot off the ship all day. Even as we motored south now, keeping the east coast of Spitsbergen on our starboard beam, and as the light began to fade slightly, the excitement was yet to build again.

Over the tannoy came the soft Orcadian notes of Martin's voice: 'Ladies and gentlemen. Before we head further south for Sørkapp, we are going to see if we can get a little closer to this second bear.'

I glanced across at Mick.

'Didn't know that there was a second bear.'

'Me neither!'

We swung our camera bags onto our backs, turned from the lovely little ivory gulls, and ran down the side decks to the bow.

There we discovered a dozen or so of the passengers, plus a couple of the crew. Dead ahead was another bear, smaller than the last, and perhaps 500 yards away.

'This individual is probably a female,' said Martin. 'She may well have a cub to feed and is definitely hunting,' came over the tannoy.

The bear seemed a little unsure of the ship and for a moment looked as though she was going to run towards the land. The captain again ordered his crew to cut the engines, and just as the bear seemed to be about to make off, she turned again towards us and stared.

She held position for a couple of minutes and then lost interest in the great block of metal that had appeared through the ice. She began sniffing the ice and then almost immediately raised herself up onto her hindlegs and came down hard, pounding the ice in front of her with her front paws close together. She repeated this and was obviously trying to break a hole in the pack. Another pounding, and we saw a spurt of cold water rise from the hole. The bear stuck her head through the new opening, held it there for a few seconds, then withdrew. She stepped a few yards to the side and began to repeat the process.

In the meantime the glaucous and ivory gulls had begun to show an interest in the hunting antics of the bear – scavenging is the chief source of food for both of these gull species, and the bear provides plenty of scraps for them to gather when it has caught its prey. Three glaucous gulls examined the hole which the bear had now given up on, while five ivory gulls floated overhead. Another glaucous gull seemed much more interested in what the bear was doing now and got very close to her as she began pounding on the ice again. The great bear rose, then slammed down hard. She rose again as if to repeat the punch, but as she came down, and with admirable agility for such a large creature, she twisted towards the gull and made to grab it before it could fly away. The gull squawked, turned awkwardly with the primary feathers from its right wing caught in the dagger-like claws of the bear's paw, then pulled free as feathers flew into the air.

The bear, having missed a meal of glaucous gull, now seemed to lose interest. She turned away, and, without even a single glance back at the *Grigoriy Mikheev* and her startled passengers, she trotted, almost daintily, across the ice for a quarter of a mile.

We watched avidly to see what she would do next. The bear stood for a few minutes and then slowly began to sniff the ice and snow at her feet. She quickly rose into the air and resumed her strange hunting strategy as the captain fired up the engines, and we motored on southwards leaving the great ice bear to find herself a meal on the frozen shelves of the Storfjorden.

High winds blew in from the west overnight. For the first time during the voyage I had an uncomfortable night's sleep. The ship seemed to be listing wildly to the starboard side throughout much of the sunlit night, and I could hear things rolling around in my small shower room. I got up to track down the wayward soap dish, deodorant bottle, or whatever, but couldn't see anything that might be making a bid for freedom in the tiny cubical. Just as I was getting back into bed, I heard the noise again, a swift scraping, then a dull thud. I guessed it was something in the next cabin. I turned my pillow to the other end of the bunk so that my feet were downhill against the tilting of the ship, rather than my head, and got a fitful few hours of sleep.

The following morning brought a slackening in the wind, and as we were heading into one of the huge sheltered fjords on the west coast of Spitsbergen, it seemed likely that we'd be completely out of the wind once we were amid the mountains.

After breakfast I wrapped up warmly – this involved donning several layers, starting with two thermal tops. On top of this I wore two fleece sweaters, then a Torres waistcoat that Paramo had given me to test. Finally, an over-the-head Torres smock, also from Paramo, and my top half was ready for the Arctic. My legs have always been fairly warm, so a single pair of thermal bottoms acted as a base layer beneath a normal pair of walking trousers. On top of this I pulled on either my waterproof salopettes, to keep out the wind more than anything, or a pair of thickly padded, windproof trousers, again from Paramo. If it was really cold, I wore both! A pair of fleece gloves for my hands and a mountain hat for my head, and I was ready for anything.

This all seemed a little over the top at times, but these clothes meant that I could stay comfortable on deck for long periods of time, while all the other passengers only managed the odd hour here or there before rushing off for the warmth of their cabins. I simply didn't want to miss anything – I'd come to the Arctic to see the wildlife, and at least while the sun shone, I would be damned before I'd let the intense cold send me scurrying off below deck.

Once I was up on the monkey deck, I saw that a startling array of pointed peaks, thrusting out of pure white glaciers, was ranged on all horizons. While I'd been preparing myself in my cabin, dressing and grabbing camera and binoculars, the captain had steered the *Grigoriy Mikheev* deftly into the deep fjord of the Hornsund. Huge seracs towered over the ship, hanging in white meringues from the peaks themselves, while the snouts of the sparkling glaciers, shining blue as the sky reflected through the frozen water, threatened to calve bergs the size of double-decker buses into the tranquil waters.

The plan for the morning was to go out in the Zodiacs on a mini-cruise through the shattered ice floes that fringed the bay itself, filling the head of the fjord. I found myself in a boat operated by Mick, and, together with another eight or nine passengers, he pushed the boat gently through the shallow rafts of ice.

Way out over the flatness, 50-odd harp seals basked by the edge of an opening in the floe, but Mick knew that he'd not be able to get the tiny craft close enough to them for us to get good views, and besides, if he'd tried they would have just flopped into the water and disappeared anyway.

As we moved away from the *Grigoriy Mikheev*, we could get a strong appreciation of just how big these mountains around us were. The ship looked almost toy-like as she nestled at anchor beneath the jagged fingers of red rock of Hornsundtind, the 1,431-metre peak on the west side of the subsidiary fjord we were exploring, and we could also see Martin's Zodiac chugging towards this stupendous mass of mountain architecture with its diminutive cargo of passengers. At this distance his boat was just a minor speck in the startlingly vast landscape of ice and snow, and we had to use binoculars just to see that it was indeed him at the helm.

Mick Brown at the helm of his Zodiac in the Hornsund

The east shore of the fjord rose in gentler slopes to the rounded, snowy whale-backs of Påskefjella, not that dissimilar to the fells of the Skiddaw range in the Lake District, or perhaps the Monadh Liath mountains of the Scottish Highlands. The obvious and all-too-noticeable difference here was the long line of bear prints in the snow just above the waterline. It looked as though the bear had been hunting along the edge of the fjord, probably hoping to catch a seal off guard. The tracks dipped regularly right down to the shore and then climbed in shallow curves away from the edge of the water ice. Mick cut the engine and we scanned the slopes above, looking for the bear itself. This time, however, we were not as lucky as we had been the previous day – there was no sign of the animal on the vast snow slopes above our tiny rubber boat.

On one ice island in the middle of the fjord we found a small group of black guillemots at rest. These watched us slip by, and then as we headed away from them, they slithered off the ice like penguins and dived beneath the surface of the water. A rising spiral of bubbles showed beneath the calm surface, just a few feet away from our Zodiac, and then the three birds bobbed up like corks. They were obviously very intrigued by the passing craft and followed us for a while, occasionally opening their bills to show the bright scarlet gape within.

I asked Mick if we might see any more little auks before the end of the trip. We'd been shown some at a distance back on Jan Mayen and had since seen plenty flying by the ship as we'd continued with our journey northwards, but so far we'd not managed to get near enough to the tiny birds for me to photograph them.

Mick just smiled, 'If we're lucky we might see a few this afternoon. But that would be our last chance.'

Almost immediately a flock of about 35 little auks passed by in the direction of the Hornsundtind on the other side of the fjord. Close behind them 12 Brunnich's guillemots flew through towards the same destination. All, however, still tantalisingly beyond the reach of my camera lens.

The other bird I really had expected to see on Spitsbergen was, of course, the barnacle goose. So far I'd not seen a single one, but as all the land we'd seen during our brief few hours on the whole of the Svalbard archipelago had been snow covered, I was not particularly surprised by this.

A couple of Arctic skuas filed by as we made our way back to the ship, and a dark scimitar flashed briefly across the crenellated north ridge of the Hornsundtind, high above the fjord. My immediate impression was 'peregrine', but I thought I'd read somewhere that birds of prey were almost absent from Svalbard, and so wanted to doublecheck this with Mick. He said that to his knowledge the only raptors were the occasional gyrfalcon, and even those were rare. I told him about the bird I'd just seen, but my peregrine theory was quickly dismissed. 'Probably a raven,' Mick thought.

Back on board, the crew were quick to draw in the anchor, and we began the short cruise back into the main sea inlet of the Hornsund. At the far eastern reaches of this huge fjord, known here as the Brepollen, a number of creaking glaciers swept down to the shore, and the captain brought the bow of the *Grigoriy Mikheev* right up underneath the crowning wall of rotting ice of the Hornbreen Glacier. Here, pinnacles of ancient ice threatened to peel off into the sea, and Martin and Mick both looked horrified as the captain edged closer and closer to the ice face.

A member of the ship's crew was sent forward to the bows and was instructed by radio to touch the wall of ice when we were within reach. I could see Martin visibly sweating, and, shaking his head in dismay, he asked the captain to put a message over the tannoy requesting that passengers didn't go forward to emulate the crew. Clearly the captain saw this little feat as a show of his great prowess as a mariner. Fortunately, once the crew member had reached out a shaky hand to touch the gleaming wall of ice, a wall that could have crumbled upon him at any moment, and would surely have meant certain and instant death, Captain Aleksandr saw this as a job well done and immediately backed off.

One of the many interesting things about this particular part of the island of Spitsbergen is that the glaciers here provide a short through route from the west coast at Brepollen to Hamburgerbukta on the east coast. It is believed that the name Hornsund itself comes from the English 'Horn Sound', indicating that this through route may once have been a sea channel from one coast to the other, rather than just the dead-end bay that we could see as we motored around Brepollen.

Wonderful snowy peaks at Brepollen on Spitsbergen

When the early explorers came in here in the early 1600s, there could well have been less ice in this bay then, as it is known that the following centuries generally had slightly colder mean temperatures. During this intervening period, in what has since become known as 'the little ice age', the ice could easily have built up to completely block the sea passage. This cold snap peaked in the early 19th century. In more recent times radar measurements have been taken to try to establish whether there is land or sea beneath the glacier itself, but still the question has not been solved. It seems that the instruments used to measure ice thickness have a slight margin of error, and scientists can't agree on whether the land under the ice lies just beneath the water surface or just above it.

Harp seals lounged sleepily on slabs of ice that had recently tumbled into the drink, and some of these slabs had become wedged on those just below the surface, many with discoloured tops and sides from the silt that had been ground down beneath the weight of the glacier itself. The seals ignored us completely, not even bothering to raise an eyelid as we floated smoothly by.

On the north side of the Hornsund lies yet another huge inlet, the Burgerbukta, and again this fjord was ringed by mighty cliffs. The peaks of the Storbreen rose majestically straight out of the dark depths of the fjord to the east, while to the west a vertical wall of rock formed a foreground to the Hansbreen range.

More guillemots came tumbling from the cliffs here, and little auks joined them in their thousands from off the sheer Hansbreen cliffs. I followed a group of these with my binoculars, noting that further out, back towards the main fjord of the Hornsund, huge numbers of birds piled into the various nesting cliffs on all sides.

Then I spotted that some of these birds were noticeably larger than others, and with a bit of careful twiddling with the focusing, I could now see about 20 barnacle geese winging in over the voe. At last, Svalbard's population of geese had revealed itself, and I knew that there was a very good chance that I'd seen these very individuals on the Solway wintering grounds last season. Obviously I couldn't vouch for this, as 26,000 geese can cover an awful lot of Scottish merse and Cumbria marsh, but there is no doubt that these very same barnacle geese would have spent the last winter down there on the border between England and Scotland.

As we slipped out of the Burgerbukta Fjord, we clung quite closely to the north shore of the Hornsund, and as we began the slow motor westwards, out towards the open sea, I could now see a few geese actually coming off the cliffs themselves.

Our next port of call, as it were, was the Polish Research Station at a place called Isbjørnhamna, lying at the entrance to the Hornsund Fjord on its north side. Isbjørnhamna means 'Ice Bear Harbour', a telling name indeed, indicative of the regular polar bear sightings in the entire Hornsund region throughout the summer months.

The Polish began exploring Svalbard in the 1930s, concentrating their efforts mainly on glacial parts of the south of Spitsbergen. The Polish Station here at Isbjørnhamna was founded in 1957, and today has a permanent staff of nine, their numbers being swelled in the summer months to fifteen or sixteen scientists.

We landed by Zodiac on the stony shore in front of the group of huts, but not before a slightly embarrassing episode that was made even more excruciating by the way Martin handled it.

As we were heading over the calm waters in our Zodiac, a big white bird flew over our boat and I paid it little attention. Edwin and Ann-Marie, a Dutch couple who were sitting beside me, shot bolt upright and swivelled around on the rubbery gunwale on which we sat. They were following the bird with their binoculars, and I, too, spun around to try to see what had caught their attention. By this time the bird was just a white speck vanishing over a bump of shingles down on the far shore. I asked Edwin and Ann-Marie what they thought they'd seen, and Edwin, who lives on marshland in the Netherlands and sees these kinds of things every day of his life, immediately answered, 'Heron'. He made it very clear that he wasn't

Exploring the ice floes of the Hornsund on Spitsbergen by Zodiac

positive, but said that it looked very much like the white herons that nest in the willow swamps outside his back door at home.

'Seems very unlikely up here,' I explained.

'That's what I thought,' he admitted, 'but I can't think what else it could have been.'

'You should tell Martin and see if he thinks it likely.'

'No! No, I think maybe I am mistaken.'

'Well, if you're sure...'

'Oh. I don't know.' He looked puzzled.

'Describe to me as best as you can.'

'Well, let's see. White all over. Hunched neck', he glanced across at Ann-Marie for confirmation, 'and legs trailing behind.'

Ann-Marie nodded and said, 'Yes, trailing legs.'

'Has to be an egret.'

'Do you think we should tell Martin?' he asked.

'Well, it could be of interest to the ornithologists who keep the records of bird sightings up here.' Still seems unlikely, I thought, but these two are no fools, and their description was bang on for an egret.

'Do you think he'll just say we're stupid?' asked Edwin.

'Possibly.'

'Oh, it doesn't matter. Probably a goose or something.'

'OK. Do you want me to tell him? I don't mind if he thinks I'm stupid!' I said.

By this time we had covered the short distance to the shore and were on the loose cobbles pulling off our waterproofs and life jackets.

I wandered over to where Martin and Mick were preparing their rifles and flares, ready to lead us on a short walk around the bay where, we had been warned, polar bears might lurk behind every boulder.

'I know this is going to sound really stupid,' I began, 'but we think we might have seen an egret flying over as we came in on the boat.'

Mick smiled and politely walked away, but Martin practically pounced on the idea. 'What did it look like? Which way was it going?'

I described what Edwin had told me he'd seen and the general direction that the bird was flying when I'd seen it flying over.

'Could be either a cattle egret, or a snowy egret,' he said confidently.

'What about a little egret?' I asked, as I knew that these birds had been shifting their range northwards with the effects of global warming, and had been nesting in England for a few years now, though previously they had been restricted to the south of France and Spain.

'No, the most likely is the snowy egret.'

'But is it likely at all?' I asked.

'No. Not a bloody chance,' he chuckled.

With that he gathered all the passengers around us and to my horror announced that, 'Graham thinks he might have spotted an egret flying over.' I grimaced as he went on, 'If so, it will be the first of its kind ever recorded in the Spitsbergen archipelago, and it seems extremely unlikely to me, but in the interests of science I insist that we all trudge over this boulder field to try to find it.'

The passengers, many of them old and frail, seemed happy with this, as they didn't know how rough the ground was going to be, so I piped up, 'I really don't think it could have been an egret. It just looked a little bit like it to me as it flew over.' But by this time I was committed, as, unfortunately, were the rest of the group.

We climbed onto a crumbling mass of boulders, the median moraine of one of the glaciers, and followed it around in a long, rough curve above the shore. Admittedly we didn't walk very far – perhaps three quarters of a mile or so – but the going was quite hard for anyone not used to walking over rough mountain terrain.

Then, as we crested a slight rise, Martin and myself out in front, I spotted a tiny white blob way out in the distance. My heart leapt. I stopped to have a quick look myself. It certainly looked like an egret through the binoculars, but it still looked a great distance away, perched on the rocky shore at the outfall of the Hansbreen Glacier.

Tentatively I stopped Martin in his tracks.

'There. On the far shore, below the dark-blue runnel of ice in the snout of the glacier.'

Martin raised his glasses to his eyes to follow my directions.

'I'm not sure if that's it or not,' I went on, 'just looks like a white bird at this distance, but it's in the direction that the other bird flew earlier, and it does look very upright like an egret.'

'It does, doesn't it,' Martin agreed.

He sat down on the scree, bracing himself against a large boulder to steady his binoculars, and leaning his rifle against the other side, then spent a good five minutes or more fixed intently on the distant bird.

Mick came up the slope to where we sat, bringing the stragglers from the group and asked what we were looking at.

'Not sure really,' I said, 'but there's a white bird over on the far shore that could be the possible egret.'

'It's not a possible egret,' chipped in Martin at last. 'It is an egret.'

He swung to his feet and began pointing out the distant speck to the rest of the group, obviously very excited.

'What kind of egret is it?' someone asked.

'Hard to say at this distance,' admitted Martin, 'but it looks most likely to be a cattle egret.'

Meanwhile Mick whispered something in Martin's ear, and, turning his back on this, the rarest ever of all Spitsbergen's bird species (obviously excluding the great auk, which being extinct is about as rare as you can possible get!), started descending the moraine on the landward side.

Martin again dropped to his position by the boulder and carefully scrutinised the white, unhurriedly moving speck through his binoculars.

Slowly he rose. 'Sorry folks,' he sighed, 'it's actually just a glaucous gull.' He looked slightly embarrassed, but eased himself out of this uncomfortable feeling by turning to me and loudly saying, 'Never mind Graham. We all make mistakes, but it really was never very likely that we'd see an egret up here in the Arctic.'

'I never really did think it looked that much like an egret anyway,' he went on, 'but I thought you seemed to know your birds a little bit, so I thought we'd better check it out.'

With that, he swung his rifle over his shoulder and stomped off down the moraine after Mick, leaving us to catch up as quickly as we could. Obviously, his feeling of embarrassment over our misidentification was stronger than his desire to keep an eye out for us and the possible attack from polar bears.

There was a small snow slope to be descended, and I showed the group how to glissade down this, which basically meant that they sat in the snow and slid down on their bums, using the concave nature of the large drift to slow their slide as they gained the bottom and reached the flatter ground and softer snow that lay there. This also speeded the whole procedure up, and we soon caught up with our two guides and the protection of their guns.

Over tundra, all orange, green and red with spongy mosses, and through the odd patch of snow, we came to a rough slope of broken scree and moss topped by layered slabs of rock.

As we approached, the air came alive with hundreds of thousands of birds, black and white flicking lightly through the blue sky on short, wildly flapping wings. We walked a short way up the slope, towards the base of the scree slope on which this entire colony of little auks seemed to be nesting. At last, I thought, I'm going to get close to these wonderful tiny birds.

We made a pile of gear by a couple of boulders at the base of the scree slope, and Martin explained that he would sit there and keep an eye out for bears if we all wanted to climb up the slope to get close views of the birds. They were very confiding, he said, and were apparently not at all worried about the presence of a human at the entrance to their burrow nest. All we had to do was climb up the slope to a likely spot, and just sit there and wait, letting the birds come back to their nests.

Some people opted to just wait with Martin while a dozen or so of us fanned out up the scree, snow and moss slope. I went for a direct approach to an area that I could see was already bristling with auks. As I climbed I took a few insurance shots with the camera, in case they took off and didn't come back, but the delightful little mites just sat there and watched me climb. I passed within a couple of feet of a bunch of them, and all they did was shuffle round slightly on their boulders to get a better view of me.

This was truly wonderful – the very thing I'd come to the Arctic for. Not necessarily little auks, but to immerse myself in its wildlife and to get up close and personal with exciting species like this.

The birds wheeled in big arcs across the skies, while others shuffled hither and thither across the stony flank of the mountain. Pairs mated on rocks and on the snow slopes either side, while others dipped in or out of the nooks and crannies beneath the stone on the scree slope, checking out suitable nesting sites or possibly revisiting old ones. I clicked away with my camera, aware that I would probably never get a chance like this again.

I'd heard that the little auk is possibly the most numerous seabird in the world, a title also sometimes pinned to the Wilson's storm petrel, and with the numbers of birds here on the scree slope above the scattered huts of Isbjørnhamna I could well believe it. One thing is for certain, these are by far the most numerous of the auk species in the Arctic, with a breeding population of well over a million pairs in Greenland, and at least a staggering 10 million breeding pairs in Svalbard. That's a minimum of 20 million little auks nesting on the rocky scree slopes around the archipelago, and you could probably add about half that number again to account for birds nesting on inaccessible cliffs that haven't been surveyed, and also non-breeding individuals.

Staggering though these figures are, I was very keen not to get too completely engrossed in the delightful, and yes, I have to say it, incredibly cute little auks, and to try also to take in my surroundings, for being halfway up a hillside overlooking one of the most spectacular fjords in the Norwegian Arctic, this certainly was a wonderful viewpoint.

Beneath me I could see Martin's little base camp at the bottom of the slope, while a little further away I could make out the red-walled timber buildings of the Polish Station. In the bay beyond that the *Grigoriy Mikheev* lay calmly at anchor, forming a perfect focal point for the amazing ring of snowy Arctic peaks that rimmed the Hornsund.

A small herd of reindeer, just a group of five, came down the hill to my left as I looked out across the scene, clicking down the snow slopes to a patch of lush vegetation where they immediately began to graze.

Then, from the layered rock slabs above where I sat, a braw cackling honk carried over the still air. I looked up and suddenly realised that there were barnacle geese flying in and out from the cliffs and higher scree slopes.

I was sitting beneath one of the biggest barnacle goose nesting grounds in the Svalbard archipelago, and I knew that within the next few days these birds, my Solway geese, would be laying eggs on inaccessible ledges and scree fringes. A pair passed over, honking to each other to keep contact, then winged out over the Hornsund and were lost to sight, while others came in and vanished onto the slopes above.

Spectacular rock pinnacles
surround Hornsund on
Spitsbergen

I had always been amazed, and slightly doubtful I have to say, when I'd read
that these geese nested on mountain slopes, but here they were, right above my
head. Of course, not all barnacle geese nest in such seemingly unsuitable places,
many do nest on rocky islands and skerries out in the bay, but the key to finding a
good nest site seems to be that word 'inaccessible'. Whether this is to make it hard
for humans to reach, or perhaps bears and foxes, I don't know. I suspect probably
both. But the geese certainly go a long way in their attempt to stop predation.

I photographed some of the geese as they came in, wondering if any of these
were the satellite-tagged birds that Larry Griffin was tracking from his computer
desk back at Caerlaverock on the Solway.

In many ways it didn't really matter. These birds – in fact *all* the Svalbard birds
– were from the Solway, and I felt that I had come the full distance in my pursuit
of the birds from the Firth in winter. I took a dozen or so more shots of the geese

101

and of the little auks, and then slipped down the slope back to the group as they gathered by Martin's boulder.

Edging around a knob of rock, its crown tufted with blossoming purple saxifrage while its sides still held snow on its skirts, the reindeer spotted our little group. They stared straight at us for a few seconds then split, three rushing off to the right, heads held high in alarm, and two just putting their heads down and carrying on with their grazing, ambling slowly across the tundra as they did so.

We, too, had split. Most of the group had gone off to say hello to the 'inmates' at the Polish Research Station, while five of us had opted to go with Mick on a short walk around the tundra to see what other wildlife we could spot.

Snow buntings chirruped from rocks and an arrow of golden plovers whipped by overhead, landing at the far end of a small lagoon that lay on the oceanward side of the land away from the station. A couple of Arctic skuas, pale-phase birds looking very smart at the start of their breeding season, sat on the tops of nearby boulders looking all toffee-nosed and aloof.

Then we'd come across the small herd of reindeer and wanted to see how close we could get to them. These remaining two seemed remarkably tame, and allowed us to approach quite closely without appearing alarmed at all.

The Svalbard reindeer, which has existed on these wild islands for thousands of years, is actually a subspecies of the mainland reindeer. *Rangifer tarandus platyrhynchus* is known to be the smallest subspecies of reindeer in the world. The legs are shorter and the fur thicker than other reindeers, and a buck may grow to a length of about 160 centimetres. The buck would typically weigh around 90 kilos in the summer, and about 60 kilos in winter. Calving takes place in June on the open tundra, after a gestation period of seven months. The reindeer on Svalbard became totally protected in 1925 following many years of heavy hunting, but today hunting of a limited number of animals in the autumn is permitted. The latest population counts show that there are around 10,000 Svalbard reindeer today.

We took our photographs then trudged carefully over the delicate tundra, avoiding the flora wherever we could, to meet the others as they emerged from the station. As we jumped into the waiting Zodiacs to be zoomed back to the ship a pair of barnacle geese flew by, just 70 feet away, and for a moment I thought I might have caught a glimpse of a small satellite-tracking device. Then the goose turned slightly and I could no longer see anything other than its back end.

Still, it was a very fitting end to my journey to Spitsbergen, for the night ahead would bring the island's capital, Longyearbyen, closer, and in the morning we'd all land at the small pier west of the town and be transferred to the airport ready for our flight home.

13

Returning south

The autumn was now drawing in again. A friend from Scotland had recently moved to Norfolk, which seemed odd to me, as she was now out of what I think of as being her natural habitat.

When I first began working for Wilderness Scotland, Janet Fisher had joined the company soon after to take on the role of operations manager. Since then I'd always pictured her as sitting at her desk in their swish office in Edinburgh, busy liaising with hotel owners, Mallaig boatmen, hire-van companies or whatever. Either that or out in the hills themselves, as Janet is also qualified as a guide and managed to combine her office administration talents with getting out into the wilds as often as she could. She'd joined me a couple of times as a 'shadow' on the winter trips I run for the company, and we'd also worked together as guides on various summer trips when occasionally the groups were too large for a single guide to deal with safely.

I guess I occasionally place people in mental niches in my mind, and Janet's was definitely the Highlands and Islands of Scotland. So, as you can imagine, she threw me completely when she moved to the flatlands of Norfolk to do her Masters degree. However, I probably threw her completely, too, when I moved first to Cumbria from Scotland, then, even more bizarrely, to southern England from Cumbria, so at least we're equal on that score.

Living in the south meant that it was relatively easy for the pair of us to get together occasionally. When Janet came over to Wessex where Olivia and I had lived for a while, we'd had a great time exploring some of the archaeological remains that dot the chalky downlands of Wiltshire. We'd also managed a day's rock climbing down on the Dorset coast at Portland, so at least we were still able and keen to put our mountain skills to the test once in while.

On another occasion, as the autumn came thrusting in from the North Sea on chill Arctic winds, I headed over to Norwich to see Janet in her new habitat. She'd bought a nice little flat near the city centre, and on the first day, we ventured out to Southwold on the Suffolk coast.

Southwold itself is, of course, well known for its pretty little high street, its stunning and beautifully sweeping long beaches, and for its impressively expensive beach huts. A quick lunch of smoked-haddock chowder and a pint of Adnams Broadside in the Crown Hotel in town set us up nicely for an afternoon walk northwards towards Easton Broad, a large reedbed and saltmarsh set atop low cliffs of boulder clay and mudstones.

Grey clouds hung in dense folds across the sky, peeling apart in tiny chinks here and there to let a dab of watery sunshine through, while a cold breeze carried straight off the sea towards us from the distant wastes of the Arctic. A few turnstones and ringed plovers juggled among the pebbles on the beach, while rafts of brown-backed juvenile herring gulls and black-headed gulls, each now without their black-heads, bobbed on the choppy surf.

Golf-ball-sized holes in the clay cliffs showed where sand martins had built nests in large colonies during summers' past, while at one point during our stroll, a huge migrating squadron of pied wagtails, probably numbering 70 or more birds, and more commonly known as 'a fall', came in off the sea and set to work picking for food on the shore. These birds were obviously being carried along by migration fever and were just stopping off to fill their bellies before continuing southwards to warmer climes.

Then, as we walked, a loud 'brattle' carried towards us along the sweep of the beach. Fifty or sixty geese rose in a scruffy cluster from the farmland that sits atop the cliffs. These for me were the first barnacle geese of the season. Here was the arriving autumn, carrying down from the Arctic a returning, honking herald of the new season. The birds gained a little height, circled back over the town, then, pointing northwards, swept along the beach's curve and sailed in tight formation out of sight.

I'm not sure if the sight of these wild geese lifted Janet's spirits at all, but they sure did mine. I'd spent the best part of a lifetime enjoying wild birds, slowly learning more and more about them as the years went by, but this was the first time I'd intentionally followed the course of a year in the life of one particular species.

From Caerlaverock and Campfield Marsh on the Solway Firth to Svalbard and the Arctic, I'd traced barnacle geese through all their trials and tribulations. Watching the first of the season's barnacles return to Britain for the winter was strangely moving and exciting, even though I knew I'd probably never clapped eyes on these particular individuals before.

These would almost certainly not be geese from the Svalbard group. No, these would most likely be geese from the Russian flocks, for I knew that the Svalbard birds would be way off course if their route had brought them here to the most easterly shores of Britain. No, Svalbard's birds should by now be coming into the airspace of the Solway, while those from Greenland would be moving in skeins over the skies of Islay.

I walked on, chatting with Janet about these things, and our conversation quite naturally turned to talk of Scotland. I knew then that I'd have to journey northwards once again, and soon. To go back to the Solway to watch the geese returning from Svalbard, and to travel further north to Islay, to see the spectacle of 20,000 of Greenland's barnacle geese coming in low over Loch Indaal.

Over Easton Broad, a couple of hen harriers quartered the drifts of browning *Phragmites*, the reeds upon which their prey relies for shelter, food and, during the summer, nesting sites. A green woodpecker yaffled away from the depths of an old oak wood on the far side of the broad, while a skitter of ringed plovers still worked their way busily along the shore. But my mind was in the north – I knew Janet understood this, as she often feels the same way – and I knew I'd have to start planning a trip to Scotland as soon as I got home.

That wasn't the last we saw of the geese off the East Anglian coast, though. The following afternoon we ventured along the Norfolk Coast Path from West Runton, a little village tucked neatly into the wooded slopes of a fine cluster of small hills, just west of Cromer. After our walk over heathland and through lovely oak and Scot's pine woods (jarring my mind, taking it back to the north yet again), we sat on a bench in Cromer enjoying the views out over the North Sea, each with a bag of fish and chips in our laps. The same brazen honking noise carried above the surf, and within a couple of minutes a skein of barnacle geese flew by, 54 of them, still in tight formation, but this time heading westwards for the confines of The Wash.

The excitement of the autumn gathering of birds in Britain had begun, as it always does at this time of year, without fail. And I just couldn't wait to get out there and to be a small part of it again, or at least to be among it as it happened.

A couple of weeks passed in a frenzy of work, but I couldn't shift from my thoughts the wildest vestiges of the Highlands of Scotland and wind-wrecked shores of the Western Isles.

Fog clothed the hills as we slipped through the calm waters of the Sound of Islay onboard the Calmac ferry, the MV *Isle of Arran*. It was now mid-November, and there was not a lot of wildlife about, either on the sea or in the air, as Olivia and I scanned around trying to spot anything interesting as we approached Port Askaig. A couple of square-headed great northern divers bobbed on the steely-grey flats of the Sound, and a flutter of black guillemots, now almost white in their winter plumage, flicked past the ferry as we slowed down nearing the pier. A raft of eiders, 'oohoo-ing' at each other, slipped from the wrack-covered rocks into the bay, bow-waving eastwards along the coast, and as we gazed inland at the rough cluster of houses scattered loosely around the rocky bay, lots of gulls sat atop the chimney breasts, gaining some meagre warmth from poorly insulated roofs.

On the face of it there seemed to be little to entice us to this wild, rugged place, other than the certainty of lots of good peaty whisky, and the possibility that the huge flocks of Greenland barnacle geese might have returned here to their wintering grounds.

Once on the island we stopped by at Caol Ila for a tour of the distillery. The whisky from this little still had been a favourite of ours for some time, although many find its slightly medicinal flavour a little off-putting. We enjoyed our private tour, and then had a nosy down at the pebbly shore to see if there were any interesting birds down there. A pair of black guillemots dived for food in the shallows, and more eiders floated by in a brown, black and white jumble.

We then drove over the centre of the island through Ballygrant to Bowmore, the main town of Islay, and the place where we would be staying. Our hotel, the Lochside, seemed hemmed in right at the centre of the high street, and at first glance didn't seem to be on the lochside at all. However, once we were shown to our room we realised what a superb position we had. Our view was filled by the stunning, wide expanse of Loch Indaal.

The light was low and all but blocked out as we hunkered beneath a dense, grey cloak of cloud. We walked out around the town, wondering if our journey to this island would bring a brighter morning and a warmer welcome to the hundreds of thousands of birds that had made a much longer journey, all the way from Arctic Greenland.

At the southern tip of Islay there is a ragged peninsula, riven by harsh winds and wild seas. This is The Oa, pronounced simply as the letter 'O'. A wildness of open moorland, crags falling in steep slopes into the broiling sea, and wasted coves of shingle and sand. The RSPB holds large acres of this headland, chiefly for the important breeding population of choughs, and we wanted to spend some time exploring in the hope that we might come across these flamboyant members of the crow family.

Choughs are basically about the size of a crow, but have bright red bills and legs, making them appear slightly comical. The first time we saw them together was over on the west coast of Ireland at the Cliffs of Moher in County Clare. Olivia had never seen choughs before and was delighted to watch the tumbling black dervishes, whirling on the updraught from the cliffs and falling in great cackling arcs across the sky. I'd seen alpine choughs before, which differ in having a lemon-yellow bill, in the Himalaya. On one occasion I'd even had a pair coming to feed on scraps from the breakfast table when I camped for a couple of weeks with a large expedition at the village of Thyanboche, below the awe-inspiring Khumbu Glacier and its attendant peaks.

Choughs are quite rare as far as corvids go. They are fairly common in Ireland, and there are a few in Wales on Anglesey, in Pembrokeshire and at Craig yr Aderyn below the mountain fastness of Cadair Idris. They have also been nesting again in

Cornwall over the past few years, much to everyone's delight, while in Scotland the only place you will find them is on Islay. I understand that there is a healthy population on the Isle of Man, but I am ashamed to say that that is one part of the British Isles that I have not yet visited.

This is a species that, at least in Britain, has a distinct westerly range, and historically the species is in slow decline. There are currently less than 500 pairs of choughs in Britain, making it a species of great concern to wildlife organisations.

The chough was once widespread around the coasts of Britain, but by the turn of the 19th century, their numbers had begun to dwindle and its range was contracting to the western strongholds. Changes in farming practices, particularly around livestock farms, as well as persecution, a word now far too often used by conservationists, are thought to be the cause of this decline in numbers. Between the years 1860 and 1900, according to the RSPB, there was a huge increase in persecution, by shooting and trapping, and as this delightful bird became more and more rare in Britain, this in itself attracted the attention of specimen hunters and collectors of birds' eggs. Choughs became extinct in most parts of England, although a few pairs clung to an existence on the cliffs of Cornwall until 1952.

Recent surveys have shown that the species is recovering slightly in parts of its range, particularly in Wales and the Isle of Man, while the Islay birds have very mixed breeding years. The RSPB is particularly worried about the choughs in Northern Ireland, as only one breeding pair has been located since 2002. The Cornwall pair, however, is still going strong, and still nest successfully. In 2007 they were joined by another nesting pair, and there is a chance that there may be three pairs present during 2008.

We parked up in the tiny bay at the end of the road, just short of Upper Killeyan farm. The windscreen wipers swiped back and forth across the curved pane, and the vehicle itself swayed violently in the wind.

Olivia and I looked at each other and laughed. Already the windows were steaming up from the warmth of our breath on the inside, while the coldness of the northerlies skimmed by outside. It seemed unlikely that we'd want to be out in the wild weather too long but were still keen to get out at least for a quick blast.

I nipped out to the boot, struggling at first even to push open the door from within as the wind forced itself hard against the panel from without. I grabbed our walking boots, waterproofs and armfuls of warm clothing, and rushed back to the warmth of the interior. We struggled into our thick layers, bashing knees against the dashboard and steering wheel as we each pulled on waterproof overtrousers, laughing again at what anyone outside might think if they could see us through the steamy glass.

Walking out along the track to the farm, greying clouds scudding by not very far above our heads, it felt good to be out braving the weather, and as so often happens, the wind itself seemed to be weaker once we were out in it than it had seemed from the car just a few minutes before.

A couple of curlews were hurled across the sky, looking very out of control, but no doubt more than able to cope in the storm. The farm looked deserted. A track led up from ours through a cow-shit spattered yard to a large metal barn, and the house shrank into the landscape, camouflaged even, the same colour as the sky. Old curtains hung behind cobwebby panes, and an umbrella palm blocked the bulk of the light filtering into the front room.

A flight of redwings and fieldfares took off from a nearby rushy meadow, pelted across the broad, grey flatness above, then alighted beyond a stone wall. We walked on, buffeted slightly as the path led us out between walls festooned with moss and yellow scales. A wren dashed into a nook, while sheep baa-ed at us from the other side of a wire fence. The fence itself joined in with the harmony, backing the sheep's song with the high-pitched whine of the wind sawing against its tautness.

The path crossed fields above a burn, leading us to the south and towards the coast of The Oa. The outline of the coast of The Oa looks particularly spiky on the map, its cliffs cut by dashing burns as they tumble to the sea and slashed from beneath by the waves.

As we neared Bruthach Mòr, just half a mile or more of walking from the farm, the view opened outwards, over heathery slopes to the tops of the cliffs themselves. Then the sweep of the sea, 300 feet below, came up at the base of these same cliffs in a startlingly white foam. Even in the greyness and mist of this wild day, the white surf cut through the sea fog and seemed almost to shine. This was in intense contrast to the drab tones of the moors and the cliffs, and indeed to the sea itself, which were dulled by the poor light.

Bruthach Mòr itself is a short promontory quite a long way over the crest of the convex slopes, and from above we couldn't see it at all. However, we could just make out the steep-sided tower of Dùn Athad across the broiling waters of Port nan Gallan. Here great bastions of rock have been hewn by sea and storm into a flat-topped ridge, upon which once stood the doune, or dun, an Iron Age hill fort.

As we gazed into the murk with the binoculars, trying to pick out the dun on the summit, and the narrow arête, which we had been told, connects it to the hillside, the wind pushed us around the slopes of Bruthach Mòr, making it very difficult to focus on anything much across the bay. I had to yell into the hood of Olivia's jacket to make myself heard above the roar of the sea and the wind.

'My binoculars are steaming up,' I yelled. She just nodded.

'Can't see much,' I tried again, 'just a few crows and gulls.'

Olivia nodded again, began to lift her binoculars, then stopped and glanced back at me.

I realised immediately what I'd just said. 'Crows' could mean a number of things. It could mean the common carrion crows that we get down in England or the rarer hooded crows of the Highlands and Islands. It could also mean rooks, which seemed unlikely, or ravens, which would have been great to see out here, but again seemed unlikely given that we'd watched maybe six or seven of the dark corvids dashing along with the wind. No. What 'crows' meant to the two of us up there on that broken cliff-top on Islay in winter just had to be something much more exciting. 'Crows' could only mean 'choughs'.

And there they were, all red-legged and brash. Not struggling against the wind, but working with it. Using the immense gusts to twist and turn across the craggy faces that surrounded the bay. Two of them flew in with the wind to their backs, feathers all ruffled and inside out, then turned swiftly into its path, using its energy, its rhythms and waves, to rise across the cove. They swung down in a huge, lunging swoop, cutting obliquely through the craggy scene. We were finding it hard to stand against the wind, and Olivia actually had to hold on to my arm so as not to be blown off the cliff itself. And yet still these wonderful birds played on the wind.

Yes, played. A chap who runs a bird of prey centre in Yorkshire once told me that in his view birds never fly for fun. On the wing, he said, they are either hunting, establishing or holding territories, or attracting a mate. Although he undoubtedly knows a lot about birds, and raptors in particular, I can only think that this chap has simply never seen choughs dancing in the wind. If they could speak in a human tongue, they'd be letting out hearty and joyous 'yippees' as they flash across the skies with the wind on their backs. Ravens do the same, and I'm sure other birds must appreciate the pure joy of flight when the wind is in their favour.

Unable to hold against the icy blasts any longer, Olivia and I turned our backs to it and walked westwards, back from the cliff edge. A meadow pipit lifted from our feet as we walked, flicked through the ling heather, then dropped into a thick patch of hard rushes where it found some relief from the wind.

A broad shoulder lay at the south-westerly corner of the Oa headland, and we were pushed to the flattening where this ridge dipped across moorland and back to the farm on our right, and rose gently to the Mull of Oa to our left. There's a monument on the highest point, a memorial to the sailors who have lost there lives at the base of these rough cliffs. Great ships have been broken here, and many men have gone to their desperate, sad, watery graves.

We stood on the shoulder, wanting to walk the quarter of a mile or so up along the wide ridge to the monument, but slightly concerned that our way would take us close by the cliff edge. Given the wind, we wondered if this would be wise. The moorland to the north-east was gentle, friendly and lay homeward, or at least car-ward. I stopped to take a couple of photographs, kneeling to lessen the effects of the wind, and when I looked through the lens towards the monument I could see that Olivia was just entering the frame on the right. She'd decided to give it a go. I took my shots then dashed across the moor to join her. We linked arms and pretty much dragged each other to the top of the hill.

Back above Upper Killeyan, just yards from the car, we stopped briefly to watch a falcon glide along, just a few feet from the ground. By now the wind had abated a little, and we could lift our glasses and watch the swift and easy course of the peregrine as he made first to a stone wall, perching briefly to gaze around at his territory, then off across the moor towards the ramparts of Dùn Athad.

At the broad entrance to Loch Indaal, south of Laggan Point, the long, white flats of the Laggan Bay sands stretch for over six miles. We stopped by the little cove at the southern end, by the farm at Kintra. Oystercatchers probed the fields, and another small jest of choughs flung themselves along the dunes. I don't really suppose the collective noun for choughs is a 'jest', but I personally feel it suits them perfectly.

Out on the sands a large black cow followed us through the surf, and as we moved up into the dunes, a grunty cackle came drifting on the wind over their marram-topped tufts.

We eased carefully to the top of the largest of these wind-driven piles of sand, feeling at times as if we were taking one step up and sliding down two. As we crested the gritty rise, there they were. Barnacle geese. Fresh from Greenland. The winter had arrived on Islay.

Islay is, of course, famous for its barnacle geese in winter. The RSPB has a huge reserve to the north of the island where many of the birds gather, and we'd be visiting this area the following day, but as we drove the short distance north from Kintra back to the Lochside Hotel in Bowmore, we seemed to be suddenly seeing more and more geese, almost as if they'd arrived while we'd been blowing off the cobwebs on The Oa. By Glenmachrie, in a field of grass, a hundred or more barnacle geese grazed the crop, while as we neared Corrary Hill yet more flew in over Laggan Bay and settled in a rough meadow.

That night we settled in to the hotel bar, a dram of Caol Ila in my hand and a Lagavulin in Olivia's, and toasted the arrival of Islay's barnacle geese. Tomorrow we hoped to find more. More barnacle geese and more bird species, for we were heading for the RSPB reserve at Loch Gruinart, way up on the northern coasts of the island. And who knew what else might have been blown ashore during the wild storms of the day?

Loch Gruinart is a huge lobe of a sea inlet on the north coast of the island. It is largely flat, estuarine and sandy, and cuts southwards into the grassy pastures and meadowlands that lie between the low hills on either side. To the east of the loch rough moorland rolls away to the north-west coast of Islay. This hinterland is studded by beautiful and little-visited freshwater lochs which hold wigeon, goldeneye, teal and mallard in the winter, while the moorland itself is hunted by pairs of hen harriers and merlin.

The coast north-west of this moorland is rocky and ragged, and terminates in the wonderful dune-backed headland of Ardnave Point. Just off shore here there's a scattering of rocky skerries lying in a string parallel with the shore. Boghachan Móra's twin rocks sit at the southern end of this chain, then the various lumps and clumps of Eilean Beag follow. Sgeirean Leathann is another sizeable rocky shelf, then there's a channel before the main island of this group, Nave Island. Here there are the remains of a monastic settlement, perched just above the southern entrance to a gully that runs across the island. Many waders feed on these islands, including purple sandpipers, turnstones, redshanks, curlews, oystercatchers, and various gulls. Otters also come ashore here to bask on the rocks or to feed on shellfish plucked from the rock pools. Ardnave Point forms the western entrance to Loch Gruinart, while across the sandy flats the other entrance is formed by the impressive dunes of Killinallan Point.

Gazing out from Ardnave Point, using the telescope to bring the birds closer, we could see a dozen or more barnacle geese grazing on Nave Island, while large flocks coursed up and down Gruinart itself.

We drove back along the narrow road from Ardnave Point, making for the RSPB visitor centre at Aoradh Farm. The viewing area in the top of the barn gave extensive panoramas across the partly flooded Gruinart Flats, and here we scanned over the largest flocks of barnacle geese either of us had ever seen. First of all we'd spotted a large flock in the wet fields immediately below the barn – a flock which must have held a good 2,000 individuals – then, as we scanned further out across the Flats, we became aware of more and more birds. The whole area was an early winter gathering ground for barnacle geese.

As we looked on, delighted at finding so much wildlife spread out before us, Olivia pointed out that there were some other, different geese down there on the Flats too. I'd read on one of the information boards that were pinned to the walls downstairs in the barn that Greenland white-fronted geese also visited the reserve in the winter, and so had a pretty good idea that these must be what she'd seen. I followed her directions, both of us with eyes stuck firmly to the lenses of our binoculars, and there they were, probably 60 or 70 white-fronts, newly arrived with the barnacle geese. Superb! And there, on the pools by the edge of Tràigh Gruineart, a dozen or so swans, feeding among the reeds. The more we looked over the huge area, the more birds we saw, although from the viewing platform in the barn many of these were simply just too far away to make out exactly what species they were. We needed to get down there, on the Flats. To get in among the wildlife, to hear the geese honking, the oystercatchers screeching and the ducks quacking and whistling.

As we continued to watch, a large bird of prey came floating in on the gentle breeze. A buzzard, probably a female judging by its large size, was hunting for rabbits or carrion over the Flats.

111

Nearer at hand, in fact right below us in the farmyard at Aoradh, the RSPB has put out a number of feeders to attract the birds. House sparrows were joined by pairs of greenfinches, chaffinches and starlings. Down on the ground, below the feeders, a male reed bunting mopped up fallen seen, while a dunnock picked about among the foliage. A pair of collared doves coo-ed from the top of the barn, while a blue tit flitted in from the middle of a hawthorn bush, grabbed a seed from the feeder and flitted off again – a definite smash and grab raid by this masked bandit!

A short way back along the lane towards Ardnave Point there is a car park, and we set out on foot from there, dropping down a slope towards the Flats. The path led through scrub of hazel, hawthorn, holly and oak, and birds called and chattered quietly to themselves. A couple of wrens trilled loudly at us – so much noise for such a small bird – letting us know in no uncertain terms what they thought of our trespassing into their territory. These tiny creatures are surely the Jack Russells of the bird world, brazenly proclaiming their territory to anyone within earshot and hurling out abuse at everyone, regardless of size.

This pair in the woods of Gruinart Farm reminded us of a wren we once watched on the shores of Bassenthwaite Lake in the Lake District. That little chap was making an awful racket, machine-gunning its alarm call loudly for all to hear. We'd watched him for a while and noticed that he was actually following something unseen to us, warning it off his territory. We'd walked along the path parallel to the yelling bird, and finally caught sight of the cause of his agitation – a stoat was hunting through the willow scrub along the lake shore. That little bird was more than ready to risk his own life in the pursuit of seeing off the dangerous intruder.

We descended a flight of steps, through the wood and out onto a farm track which cut across the Flats. Straight ahead, across the track a path led down a corridor formed by two embankments, one on either side, to a hide. Inside we found a family enjoying the birds. Mum, dad and three kids shared binoculars and a telescope they'd carried down from the car park, and between them sorted out the difference between the mallards, gadwall, teal, wigeon, shovelers and pintails that studded the scrape in front of the hide.

The buzzard came floating back over the saltmarsh, and something in the distance, an unseen dashing raptor – probably a peregrine – put up a huge flock of lapwings and golden plovers. These whirled and turned in the air, flashing black and white, and then settled again just yards from where they'd taken off.

Over on the east side of Loch Gruinart rough wilderness hills of moorland rise to the broad top of Maol na Coille, and I worked across the skyline with my binoculars, hoping for a fleeting glimpse of a golden eagle, which I knew to hold a territory in the area. Folds of grey clouds moved slowly overhead, breaking occasionally to let shafts of sunlight through, filtered into what sailors call 'God's fingers'. A spectacular sight in itself, but no eagles today.

Over to the south-east, another of the many pools that bejewel the Gruinart Flats held the small flock of swans we'd seen earlier from the barn. Now we could see them much more clearly, and with the aid of our telescope, we could make out the yellow-and-black bill of whooper swans.

We left the hide, closing the hook-up windows carefully so as not to disturb the feeding birds, and walked back along the path towards the wood. As we approached the farm track that we'd crossed earlier, I spotted a rusty-brown shape in an adjacent field, and immediately ducked behind a gorse bush, dragging Olivia with me.

'I think there's a roe deer just behind this bush,' I whispered.

'Did it see us?' Olivia asked.

'Don't think so, but it might have heard us or smelt us by now.'

We grinned at each other, and I motioned with my hands that if we crept quietly around the bush anti-clockwise, we might get a good view of the deer. Before we set off I changed lenses on my camera, going for the largest I have, a rather heavy 400 mm zoom. I upped the ISO reading on the digital body to take account of the fact that I'd be hand-holding the weighty lens, then we delicately stalked out from behind the gorse.

There she was, a lovely doe, munching away at the lush grasses in the pasture. Her white 'target' tail contrasted vividly with the dark brown of her coat, and as she looked up between mouthfuls of grass, we could see the comical little white splashes either side of her mouth that we always thought made the roe deer look like it had been caught drinking milk.

She ignored us completely, even as we stood next to the gorse bush in clear view. Olivia watched through binoculars while I stalked a little nearer, using a patch of bramble briars for cover, then slowly moving over to a telegraph pole. I stood behind this, well aware that I am a lot wider than the pole I was using for cover, and steadied my camera against its shaft as I clicked off a dozen or more shots of the deer. She looked up once or twice, even staring straight down the lens itself at one point. I wondered if she might suddenly take fright and dash off across the field, but each time she simply put her head down and carried on munching.

Just yards away, and also making the most of the lush grazing on offer, a gaggle of 43 barnacle geese joined in the feast. Six more came winging in overhead, alighting at the far end of the field, then waddling over to join the bigger flock.

Happy that I'd taken all the shots of both the roe deer and the barnacle geese I could possibly need, I just stood for a minute or two and watched the deer eat, then I slowly backed off to where Olivia was still watching in delight. Keeping an eye on the doe we both walked away, leaving her to her feeding, both of us enthralled by yet another wonderful close brush with nature.

One bird I'd really wanted to get close views of while we were on Islay was the purple sandpiper. When I was first getting interested in wildlife as a child I'd learned that these rotund little waders could be found on the harbour walls at Bridlington during the winter months, and I'd made a point each year of journeying up to the off-season seaside town to see them. I'd always been amazed at how tame these birds were and how close I'd been able to get to them as they picked along the harbour walls. The other thing that had amazed me was how all the other passers-by – dog walkers, off-season holidaymakers, early-morning newspaper buyers, shoppers and the like – all ignored the birds completely. I remember one chap with his wife asking what I was photographing on one occasion, and when I pointed out the remarkable little bird to them, explaining that it had just arrived from the Arctic where it nests on the tundra, they'd both given me a look that clearly said 'lunatic', and shuffled off to the nearest fish-and-chip shop without another word.

It had been years since I'd seen purple sandpipers close up, and I had read that the rocks in front of the distillery at Bruichladdich were the most likely place on Islay to see these birds in the winter.

After leaving Loch Gruinart, we decided, since there were still a couple of hours of daylight left and the weather was getting brighter by the minute, to drive down the west side of Loch Indaal to Bruichladdich.

Olivia spotted the purple sandpipers first, in among a small flock of ringed plovers and dunlin. There were just three sandpipers there, while dozens of ringed plovers scurried about the shore, and fourteen dunlin stood each hunched on one leg on a bank of shingle. An individual red knot, now grey in its winter plumage, plucked crustaceans from the sand, and a pair of grey herons flapped noisily by.

Out on Loch Indaal itself, rafts of eiders merged with a few common scoters and scaup, sea ducks happily feeding together. There were quite a few geese out on the sea loch, too, and at first we just assumed that these were either barnacle geese or white-fronts, as these were the only two species we'd so far seen on Islay, but as we left Bruichladdich and began the drive around the head of the loch back to Bowmore for the night, I caught sight of a gaggle of something different again down on the shore at Gortan.

They were pale-bellied brent geese, and we pulled in on the roadside to have a closer look. These were birds from the western race of brent geese, *Branta bernicla hrota*, which breed in the East Canadian High Arctic, Greenland and Svalbard, and looked quite different from the many dark-bellied western Siberian brents I had seen on the Humber over the years.

During our last breakfast at the Lochside Hotel in Bowmore, we'd sat by the window with a fine view over the levels of Loch Indaal. Turnstones and oystercatchers picked through the kelp and wrack just below the window at which we sat, and 20 or more dunlin crammed onto the partly submerged rocks that form the entrance to the tiny harbour. We watched mergansers and eiders diving in the deeper water just off shore, and large numbers of sea ducks passed by further out on the loch. We'd seen all of these birds each morning as we'd eaten and had marvelled at the huge flocks of barnacle geese that were still arriving each day from Greenland, winging in broken 'V's out of the skies and splashing onto the loch itself.

On this last morning there were 16 brent geese in the compact cove right outside our window, exactly the same number as we'd watched last night at Gortan over on the far side of Loch Indaal. This was undoubtedly the same flock, and we enjoyed the spectacle of them feeding in the shallow bay as we tucked into our breakfast before checking out and heading to Port Ellen for the ferry back to the mainland.

Just a few days before tentatively sending the manuscript for this book off to Dr Keith Whittles, my publisher, I'd decided to take one last trip north to Cumbria. I'd been commissioned by another publisher to compile a book of photographs on the Eden Valley, and planned to make a photographic journey along the length of the Eden from its source high on Mallerstang Edge right down to the sea on the Solway Firth.

From a base at the Appleby Manor Hotel, I ventured out with my camera each day, starting high in the bleak fells. On the final day of my visit to Cumbria, I set off soon after a hearty breakfast and made my way first to Rickerby Park in Carlisle. I clicked off a few shots of the River Eden as it gloops over The Swifts, then returned to my car and followed the last few meanders of this mighty river as it emerges from its confining channel and spreads out over the vast mudflats of the Solway basin. The sun beat hard from a cold winter sky, and oystercatchers, curlews and a bunch of large gulls paddled along the shoreline.

I drove west, stopping frequently to photograph the broad landscapes, as well as more minute details like mud rippled on the flats and brimming channels of water flooding off the surrounding fields and spewing into the Solway. Then, along the breadth of Burgh Marsh, a black-and-white herd of geese picked among the verdant grasses. I pulled up abruptly and got my binoculars trained on the birds. A broad smile crossed my face as I gazed at perhaps 300 Svalbard barnacle geese. I watched from a lay-by at the cattle grid just by Dykesfield as the birds rose, just a few at first, into the clear sky. These flighty few swung off to the east, then a few minutes later, passed back over the feeding flock and followed the shore westwards. As they passed, the rest of the flock became agitated and took to the air too. They wheeled across the marsh, turning sharply in a flash of black and white, and vanished into the western marshes.

I gunned the engine and drove onwards to where the road rises slightly at a junction with the lane to Boustead Hill. I stopped here on the flats just before the hill, got out and walked to the brow of the hill to get a better view over the levels of the marsh.

More oystercatchers, a score or more lapwings, and perhaps 40 golden plovers fed down by the waterline, but no sign of the geese. A mile or so further west along the road is another slight rise at the Easton junction, and I repeated my scanning manoeuvre once I got there. There's quite a deep but very narrow channel just off the roadside here, cutting through Easton Marsh and into the main vein of the Eden channel. It's a few miles from here going downstream at low tide to where the waters of the Eden meet those of the Esk amid the mudflats at a point called Bowness Wath, and I could easily see with my binoculars across the waters all the way to the confluence.

Way out, almost as far as Bowness Wath, a vast flock of birds could be seen winging through the air. At first it was hard to make out the direction the flock was flying in, let alone the type of birds these were, but as I watched intently, the distant black dots slowly became black, white and grey barnacle geese, and I could now make out the entire flock, perhaps 1,000 strong. I could see that they were heading directly for me. I rushed back to the car for the camera and clicked off a dozen or more shots of these great, wild creatures of the Arctic as they passed by me yet again, alighting on the fringes of Easton Marsh in a flurry of grey wings.

Perhaps these were some of the same birds I'd watched so rapturously from the boulder fields above the Polish Research Station at Isbjørnhamna on Spitsbergen's Hornsund. Of course, I would never know for sure, not without actually getting closer to the birds and checking to see if I could catch a glimpse of tracking devices or leg rings, but I didn't want to do that as it would have disturbed them again.

I also didn't want to take away any of the mystery of these incredible wild birds, and I knew that apart from anything else, my journey had now come to a very satisfying end.

I had followed the barnacle geese last year during their wintering on the Solway, and then as they migrated northwards, I travelled behind them up across the seas of the north to their savage breeding grounds in the High Arctic. And now, back on my own beloved Solway Firth, the geese had returned, as they always do, and I hope they will always continue to do so. They're back simply to while away their time during the balmy British winter on this wild and beautiful shore.